Seven Months Deep

Seven Months Deep

Jon King

iUniverse, Inc.

New York Lincoln Shanghai

Seven Months Deep

iUniverse, Inc.

For information address:
iUniverse, Inc.
2021 Pine Lake Road, Suite 100
Lincoln, NE 68512
www.iuniverse.com

Front and back cover design by Jon King
Front and back cover photographs taken by Breanna Hunter
Senior editor: Brian King
Editorial contributions by Ellen James and Breanna Hunter

ISBN: 0-595-32829-6

Printed in the United States of America

For Brian and Bre

JON A KING
Somewhere in Texas

OBJECTIVE
Seeking a full-time position that will utilize and build upon my skills in management, finance, statistics, and business strategy

EDUCATION
2000 to 2003: Southwest Texas State University, San Marcos, TX
Masters of Business Administration (MBA)

1996 to 1999: The University of Texas at Austin, Austin, TX
Bachelor of Arts in Anthropology, Minor in Spanish

PROJECT EXPERIENCE: Southwest Texas State University, 2001–2003
Managed a six-member team project to design and complete a business plan for World Artisans, an import retailer.

Evaluated various fictitious businesses based on forecasting methods using Excel, Crystal Ball and Process Model.

Designed a model to forecast music sales based on artist characteristics and lyrical content.

WORK EXPERIENCE
Summer, 2003: *Mojo's Daily Grind*, Austin, TX
Developed a marketing plan aimed to increase sales volume for an independent coffee shop.

2002: *Graduate Research Assistant*, Southwest Texas State University
Statistically analyzed agricultural changes in Texas borderlands related to NAFTA.

1999 to 2002: *Tour Manager*, Suntrek Adventures, Santa Rosa, CA
Led expeditions for over 200 international clients throughout the United States, Canada, and Mexico. Managed groups, organized all activities, delegated responsibilities, and translated languages.

Sometimes the creative process is more important than the final product.

For what you are about to read, that may be true. This book chronicles my experiences and thoughts during a rough period in my life. Not nearly as rough as some people of the world experience, like the struggle for basic human survival or anything like that. In fact, it sounds silly when I describe the inability to find employment as a rough period—but honestly, it was really fucking rough. During this depressing and frustrating period of my life, I undertook this project with the sole, selfish intention of making me feel better; forcing me to be productive and giving me a goal to work toward. I had no idea if anyone would ever read this, and if you are, I hope that my perspective and experiences can somehow shed some light on your own.

This project was made possible by several people. Brian King, Ellen James, and Breanna Hunter for free editing contributions. Breanna, for the continued loving support through these frustrating times. For the inspiration from dynamic entrepreneurs such as Siphon Man. Finally, for the ridiculous companies that persistently would not add me to their payroll. I sincerely thank you all for helping me realize this project.

My life's a culmination of my past achievements; all the heavy lifting all the deep breathing

—Lyrics Born, from the song *Later That Day*

Looking for a job is some time consuming, frustrating shit. It is like having the worst full-time job ever except that in this job, not only do you not acquire any skills, you don't even get paid. Job hunting is monotonous and, if endured long enough and with a sufficient amount of rejection, can be very damaging to the human psyche. Seven months after graduating with a master's in business, I spent eight hours a day, five days a week, searching for a job; just a job.

Throughout my search, I submitted over two thousand résumés and cover letters, directly to the inboxes of human resource workers and other job recruiters. I made tons of cold calls to businesses in various industries and in different cities. I visited dozens of human resource offices. The results were disappointing, far beyond disappointing, they sucked. With each day, my professional goals became lower and lower as I became increasingly more and more desperate to do anything. The hungrier you are, the less demanding your stomach tends to be.

I worked my network. I reached out to everyone I knew, including folks that I was barely knew, in hopes that someone, anyone, could provide me with a useful lead for a job opportunity. After exhausting my entire personal and very limited professional networks, the only offer that I had to show for those efforts was a three-day gig as a part-time substitute teacher at a small private school owned by a friend.

The most baffling aspect of all was that I had a fairly well groomed résumé and could enter a variety of industries seemingly easy. I have an undergraduate degree in anthropology from a prestigious university, as well as a master's degree in business. I have a lot of experience working on several business projects and have taken the lead in many of them. My professional background spans several diverse industries: I was a social worker for the betterment of migrant farm workers, an adventure tour guide for international tourists all across North America, a language translator, market researcher, statistical analyst, cashier, server and tutor. All I wanted to do was work. It was extremely frustrating that I could not get a job. It was like I was a driver; slowly approaching the highway from the entrance ramp but nobody would allow me to merge in. I knew that once I was finally able to enter the highway I'd go right to the fast lane; passing and out-performing ninety percent of all others on the freeway. But until I was granted access, I just had to sit and wait my turn. Seven months is a long fucking time to wait.

I was desperate. Not only did I need to work to provide an income stream for the most basic of things like food, rent, and gas, but I had to pay back the pile of cash that I borrowed from the state to fund my education.

The situation adversely affected my emotional state. An array of negative emotions had sunk their sharp fangs into me. The routine of consistent rejection made me depressed, angry, and apathetic. The months were a cruel experiment on the effects of chronic unemployment on the human male psyche. I had gone from confident and secure to doubtful and ineffective. Although my feelings of anxiety and depression stemmed partially from the fact that I didn't have a desk to sit at and a paycheck every couple of weeks, my feelings stemmed from the fact that I was missing out on an identity, a purpose.

There is an inherent quality imbedded in our psychological and economical systems that tells us that we need to produce. There is value, personal and economical, in being productive. Human beings have a driving need to feel that we have a value. I absolutely hated the fact that I had no income and nowhere to go during the day. For seven months my daily routine had deviated little from the following: waking up, drinking coffee, and sitting at my computer researching and applying for jobs.

The stock market crash of 1929 and the subsequent Great Depression yielded some fucked up results. Businessmen were jumping out of their office windows to kiss the pavement because when faced with the difficult reality of no income and no possible job, they chose suicide. Many of those that didn't have windows to jump from chose to pretend to work. They continued to the leave the house everyday at 8 a.m. with briefcase in hand while pretending to work at a job that no longer exists. They would spend the day at the park inventing anecdotes to tell their wives and children. We are so tied into the idea of working that we chose death and denial when without it.

Our great drive to be a part of the workforce is embedded in our minds. If we lacked the drive to hunt and gather, we would cease to have energy for our bodies, we would cease to exist. Work is hunting and gathering. In an economy that trades goods and services for money and money for food, work has just introduced a more efficient way to gather berries. The drive to work has enabled humans to survive and reproduce for generations. You wouldn't be reading this if your ancestors hadn't been driven to work.

On May 10th of 2003, I walked across the stage of Southwest Texas State University for the recognition of my completion of an advanced degree in business. My parents, my brother, my girlfriend, and some other close friends attended to show their support and pride on this occasion. When I graduated, I was excited to be finished with school and I was eager to see what opportunities would come my way.

Initially, I wasn't overly concerned about getting a job because I was certain it would only be a matter of time. It was only three months prior to graduation when I seriously started searching for jobs. When I walked that stage I figured that it wouldn't be too long before the offers began rolling in.

I couldn't have been more wrong.

I began writing this in the following October, exactly seven months since the beginning of my job search, and I was still looking. During that time, my self-esteem was taken on a roller coaster ride. Contingent on momentary employment prospects, my emotional state shifted from elation to confusion, depression to hope, anger to optimism. The fluctuation in my mood was triggered by something so seemingly insignificant, but in fact paramount: finding a job.

I felt happy when I had an interview lined up. I felt confused when I didn't get offers after I kicked ass in interviews. I felt angry when I talked to recruiters and interviewers for jobs where my skills were more than sufficient but considered not seasoned enough. After nothing but rejection it became increasingly difficult to achieve the level of confidence I once had.

The pitiful routine was affecting me so negatively and profoundly that I needed to feel productive somehow. I decided to turn my thoughts and experiences with this whole fucked-up experience into something positive: this book. Perhaps this book could be utilized as a learning tool for those fresh out of school, struggling to figure out where they stand in the world, or those simply looking for a job. Ideally, it should have value on a variety of levels, as all writings should. But most importantly, I wrote this as an outlet. Anthropologically speaking, this book makes sense. As we as humans evaluate ourselves on our levels of production, it only makes sense that I chose to use my time to produce.

A WRINKLE IN TIME

I will admit that my difficulties with the job search were partly due to my own shortcomings, but external factors definitely played a role. In May of 2003, when I graduated from *bidness skool*, the economy was at its worst in a very long time. Before I explain why, please indulge me in a brief lesson in economics.

Unarguably, humans have an infinite desire for consumption. However, there is a finite amount of resources. Economics refers to the study of who gets what and how much. The system set in place to control what and how much should be produced and consumed is known as the economy. Like ecosystems, economies are the collectives of all individuals in the specified area. The goals of an economy are to reach a point of harmony between consumers and producers, and advance the standard of living. Economies grow and shrink due to a variety of factors, but the basic reasons they fluctuate are to control purchasing power, and to value money competitively. Economies have systems of operation that control governmental involvement, business growth, and take care of their people. History has taught us that no pure system is perfect, but some systems do function relatively better than others.

One system that doesn't appear to work is communism. Communism claims that everyone has the same value and shall receive the same resources. This is a fair point; and I agree that everyone in the world needs food, medicine, safe environments, water, shelter, and access to information. Realistically though, it is human nature that we have greater relative success than our neighbors. Communism restricts this very natural desire by complete government control. Moreover, a huge problem that underlines communism is that, with all contributors receiving equal shares of the economy, there is no incentive to innovate and create. Why would an individual go beyond the call of duty if he or she knew that there would be no reward besides self-gratification?

With complete government control, consumers do not get to "vote" with their paychecks on which products and services they want. Because communistic economies disregard the theoretical framework of specialization, and therefore do not select the most efficient producers for goods, the government ends up producing expensive shit that consumers don't want. By not pushing economies and industries to concentrate all of their efforts of production on what can be produced the most efficient, communist governments may erroneously select a producer or, more likely, produce stuff themselves. Communist countries also crowd themselves out of a smooth trading environment by making trade a haphazard operation. An unfortunate side effect of a rigid communistic system is that the rudimentary means of production discourages capitalistic economies to engage in trade. The capitalistic, efficient counterparts have replaced the goods that the communistic countries provide with more scalable efficient substitutes.

Cuba is a good example of communism. Like all communist economies, it has its own set of problems and ultimately will have no choice but to become a free market in the future. Cuba, once a member of the socialist group of countries, no longer has strong trading partners. Their former partners have since altered their economic models and have converted to capitalism, not to mention the trade embargos that Cuba's enemies have placed on the Caribbean island. Again, capitalistic economies master the art of production and trade, and the trading partners specialize. If an island economy is excellent at producing oranges then that island should invest all of its energy into orange production and trade oranges for other shit from other economies. In this model, trading partners are essential. Nobody can live only on oranges.

However, Cuba is trying to do basically that. They are an island economy with few trading partners; therefore they suffer because of their self-sufficiency. A land mass as small and as limited as Cuba cannot be self-sufficient very well. Self-sufficiency is a recipe for poverty. You must trade.

I spent some time in Havana in 1998 and what I found was eye opening. I learned about places called "*casas paticulares*" where apartment owners would rent out their living space to tourists well below the cost of hotels. A couple of Swiss folks gave me the name and contact information for one in downtown Havana. When I first arrived to the island's capitol I was so excited to explore the city that I had my taxi drop me off in the middle of downtown prior to settling down in my apartment. Big mistake. I hadn't put my things up and was walking around Cuba with a big backpack, basically announcing to the world "hey, I'm not from around here, please approach me and try to sell me something." Because I was alone, people felt all the more comfortable to approach me. I would be approached by women that would flirt with me and try to make a date, and I was approached by men who would offer me the three products that Cuba had easily available on the black market: cigars, places to stay, and women. Some men would approach me from the angle that they wanted to befriend me and guide me through the town. I quickly located my apartment. The owners willingly left their home to stay with friends while I was in town, charging me fifteen bucks a night.

When I ventured back out, I was approached by some young men offering to show me around. For some reason, I wasn't up to yet another "*no gracias*," and I thought it would be interesting to hang out with some native Cubans. They told me that if the police stopped us, I should say we were all friends. Our cover story was that I had met them through a cousin who lives in Miami. With my new tour guides, I walked to the boardwalk overlooking the Caribbean. We walked a bit further and ended up in a quiet, outdoor bar. The three guys quickly ordered beer for themselves and stuck me with the bill. To them, that was the tourist-Cuban friendship. To me, I felt like a walking dollar sign. They tried their best to continue drinking and to make plans for the evening, but I managed to get away.

In the rest of my stay in Havana, I noticed many things that typify a socialistic economic model. There were no sick, starving, or homeless people. However, I did see a lot of poor people. As an island economy, there was nothing much for the people to do besides cultivate sugar and roll cigars. Kids played stickball, men played dominoes in the shade, and women danced in the streets. Stores contained an extremely limited selection of goods. Public transit consisted largely of military vehicles. Cuban citizens would look over their shoulders whenever speaking about politics and would all remind me to say that we were friends from way back. Because Cubans don't have a lot of opportunity for work, they make money however they can. They pick up musical instruments and play in the street for tips. They shine shoes. They take boxes of cigars home from the factories and sell them at a deep discount on the black market. Women sell their companionship; at least they can have food and drinks bought for them. As interesting as Cuba was, the lack of trading partners really has cut off a lot of opportunity.

Unlike Cuba, communist China plans to be an entirely free market economy by 2010. In fact, China has recognized that it is the market structure of the United States that has led to the unsurpassed advancements in technology and military. They are spending billions to emulate our achievements and have just had their first experience in space; making them fifty years behind the United States.

Then, there are capitalist systems. Capitalism allows businesses to be privately owned. Those businesses are entirely driven by the desire to make money. They make the money by selling goods and services to consumers and therefore go to great lengths to compete for that money. I am a proponent of capitalism, but I sometimes wonder if it can go too far.

Consider Wal-Mart for example. If you are one of the two people in the states that hasn't heard of Wal-Mart, let me tell you it is a huge company. They have grown with such a speed and veracity that they have bankrupted countless businesses in America and elsewhere. They have shut down a myriad of other retailers including: music stores, grocery stores, hardware stores, automotive stores, and toy stores.

The highly successful Wal-Mart business model has been one of "let's take everything that people consume and put it under one roof." Wal-Mart streamlines the consumption experience, and provides products to consumers below the prices that smaller businesses pay for the same goods at wholesale. They are able to provide the lowest prices because the scaling of the business is supernatural, Wal-Mart's are located in the outskirts of cities where property is cheaper, and they have incredibly deep pockets, enabling them to take a loss on certain products in order to profit overall. They are America's top grocer. Can you believe that? It's not even a grocery store. They purposely take a hit on the price of groceries because those shoppers are also going to shop for other shit while in the store.

What concerns me the most about Wal-Mart is that in order to charge the consumers the lowest possible prices, they have to pay their own employees shit wages and pay suppliers shit prices. This affects society in a couple of ways. For example, it widens the gap between poor folks and folks that aren't poor by having the manufacturers and employees take an earnings hit. Wal-Mart may actually help reduce the standard of living. Yes, they have cheap stuff, but they pay shit too. As Wal-Mart gobbles up other businesses, they will control too much and end up depressing the economy. What happens when Wal-Mart is the only place to shop and work?

Starbucks is another example. One of my favorite references to Starbucks is in the film *Best in Show*, when a couple is being interviewed about how they met. The wife says that they first saw each other at Starbucks, not the same one however, from adjacent Starbucks.

The Starbucks model is quite a fascinating one. They have single-handedly turned phrases like latte, barista, frappuccino, and a gang of other coffee-related terms into household words. They have branded themselves so well, that children want to drink coffee. Starbucks has created a companion, an atmosphere, and a lifestyle through their simple coffee house. They have convinced consumers that their products are the freshest and the best.

A friend of mine was recently taking a look at her bank statements and discovered something very interesting: she goes to Starbucks everyday, and when she goes she pays four bucks a coffee. Twenty bucks a week for caffeinated drinks for someone who works part-time as a nanny is quite expensive. Starbucks has successfully gained a loyal consumer base that visits them on an almost daily basis.

For its domestic growth, Starbucks has a cannibalistic strategy. It is Starbucks' goal to saturate the market so heavily that one location could possible eat into another location's earnings. For example, say there is a Starbucks on the corner of Commerce and 9th Street in downtown Austin. In the beginning, this Starbucks would dominate one hundred percent of the local coffee market by being the only provider in the area. Now imagine that a competitor started serving lattés on Commerce and 10th. The competition and differentiation would force the two businesses to share in the market (if the market was actually large enough to support two businesses). Now consider that a second Starbucks sets up another shop on Commerce and 12th. By doing so, the new Starbucks actually eats into the market share of the 9th Street Starbucks as well as the 10th street competition. Fortunately for Starbucks, they make a load of cash and can handle to lose money at one shop. They are so diversified that they are not losing money; they are only losing money at one shop, that is, until the non-Starbucks competitor can no longer afford to remain in business.

In some instances, Starbucks' strategy has proven to be counterintuitive. Another Seattle-based coffee house's expansion strategy was to open stores adjacent to existing Starbucks[1]. The competitor realized that Starbucks locations had created a consumer base for coffee. With the consumer base already in place the other coffee house would offer nothing more than healthy competition: different products, different atmosphere, and different prices. Because the competitor's strategy was a simple one, they did not have the strategic planning and market research expenditures that Starbucks had, and therefore had somewhat larger profit margins. With larger profit margins, the competitor was able to compete in a price war.

Starbucks is so successful and has spread so relentlessly that their only growth potential is now basically outside of the United States. According to a recent *Business Week* article[2], Starbucks was having problems reaching their growth goals because the U.S. business model didn't transfer directly to other countries. Other countries

---

1. "Despite the Jitters, Most Coffeehouses, Survive Starbucks In an Industry Oddity, Chain Often Gives Independents A Boost in Local Markets" by Kevin Helliker and Shirley Leung, *The Wall Street Journal*, September 24, 2002.

typically already have good coffee, and they have provided it at a lower cost than Starbucks.

The term inflation is used when the value of money diminishes. In the United States, the dollar is usually devalued by three percent every year, making goods and services three percent more expensive every year. As innovation and technology increase, production increases. That much is intuitive. As production increases, a higher amount of workers is needed to supply the appropriate quantities for the increasing demand. As more workers are employed, they are also paid, which means that those workers have increased spending power. With everybody working and producing, confidence is gained in the money markets. In time, investments are made in stocks, bonds, and other assets. When people invest in money markets and savings accounts, those institutions turn around and invest that money into other projects. With increased spending power from a greater number of people, the Gross Domestic Product (GDP) or the total money made from selling goods and services at home and abroad, increases accordingly.

As the GDP increases it raises the standard of living and increases purchasing power. When you hear that the economy grew two point seven percent last year that means that the GDP grew 2.7 percent. That 2.7 percent means that there was two point seven percent more spending than the previous year. This increased spending must be controlled so that the currency can still be used with the same weight that it had the previous year. This is accomplished by inflation. Inflation is the economy's way of keeping the GDP growth and the value of currency constant. It is regulated in a few

---

2.   "For Starbucks, There's No Place Like Home: Its overseas expansion is running into trouble" by Stanley Holmes in Seattle, with Irene M. Kunii in Tokyo, Jack Ewing in Frankfurt, and Kerry Capell in London, *Business Week*, June 9, 2003.

ways by taxes, Federal Reserve lending prices, and prices set by sellers.

If the economy grows faster than the value of currency, there can be detrimental long-term effects, including trade and supply shortages. Think about this: if everyone can buy three percent more bottles of Mad Dog, then there can be a potential shortage of Mad Dog in the market. So those that sell Mad Dog raise their prices so that they can still sell all of their supply, and earn more while doing so. Inflation becomes a problem when the price increases faster than the economy's growth.

Similarly, a recession occurs when the GDP retracts. The GDP has adverse effects when shrunken. For companies, it means that they can no longer afford the amount of employees at their current salaries. While inflation lowers the power of money, a recession increases the value of money. When money is not worth quite as much as it was the year before, consumers cannot afford as much. When consumers cannot afford as much, producers reduce their production to meet the dwindling demand. As the supply and the demand for goods reduce, the entire world economy is affected. Companies reduce their investments and in turn lay off workers. The unemployed people put their spending on hold. The workers that remain are fearful for losing their jobs and put their spending on hold too.

The result is fucked. Companies don't buy shit, which means that they don't need the workers. No workers means no jobs. No jobs means no paychecks, which means no consumption. No consumption means no production. No production means no investments. No investments means no confidence in the money markets. To remedy a recession the value of money needs to be strengthened. This is accomplished by cheaper loans and interest rate adjustments by chairman of the Federal Reserve Alan Greenspan. These are tools used to stimulate consumption and in turn can raise the GDP and eventually level out the system. In terms of international trade, a recession reduces supply, and in turn raises the price for other countries to consume our goods.

The real problem is that the effects of monetary control are not immediate. Unpredictable consumer behavior during monetary adjustments can become problematic. There is an entire area of economics dedicated to the perplexing behavior of consumers called behavioral economics. Policy makers and price setters do not make the best decisions either to stabilize currency strength or initiate consumption. If Alan Greenspan decides to lower the cost of money that banks borrow at, the increase in consumer spending may not be in the immediate future. Also, fiscal policy setters can offset taxes to either strengthen or weaken currency.

The United States does have many fortunes from being a capitalistic empire. It has created a need for innovation, production, and competition. The United States is the super power economy because private institutions are rewarded for growth and innovation. The following is what I like to call "fun with axioms."

The better the company, the more efficient the operation. The more efficient of an operation, the lower the cost of doing business. The lower the cost of doing business, the lower the cost to the customer. The lower the cost to the consumer, the higher the demand. The greater the demand, the higher the profits reaped by the company. Once a company tastes profits, the more they want to make. The more demand for output, the increased need for suppliers. The increased need for suppliers, the more jobs created. The more jobs created, the more demand and the more need for workers. Greater employment means more consumption by those with money. The increased consumption translates into increased production by producers. The more production, the more profits generated. The more profits generated, the more the competition enters the same market.

The more competitors, the more innovative, creative, socially responsible, and transparent the businesses become.

If a company gains too much power where other companies cannot compete they will have complete domination and thus be able to sell products and services somewhat regardless of the costs to the consumers. When those costs are too high only a select few can afford them. If they are necessities like electricity and food then everyone is forced to pay, thus reducing the expenditures in other sectors. This reduction in other sectors will cause less need for products and services. The reduced need will cause less need for supply and less need for workers. The layoffs will create a higher unemployment rate with people not having paychecks to buy goods and services. The anti-monopolistic policy of the United States is a good thing.

Too many employers trying to compete can also lead to long-term problems. Cost cutting is good for a consumer only if prices are really cut. Now, to further reduce costs, employers are outsourcing professional services as well as manufacturing and assembling. We have always thought of outsourcing to Third World countries in respect to factory work, but why not have Dell Computers set up offshore call centers as well? Why not outsource management? There is a clear trend of better and typically more professional positions being filled in Third World countries.

Furthermore, salaried full-time employees are declining. Due to the prices that consumers demand, companies cannot really afford to have full-time employees with benefits. So we now have temporary workers who receive neither benefits nor job security. All this is lowering America's standard of living and lowering real wages and buying power.

We are not to worry; the economy isn't that bad right now, right? Nope, it's horrible. It's not nearly as bad as some of the twenty-five percent of the world's population that live in dire poverty, or the other fifty percent that live in what we consider poverty, but we aren't doing all that great.

If you are a casual news watcher you are familiar with the relatively low unemployment rate. At the time of this writing, I believe it is about six point two. This means that for every one hundred people, seven of them (you have to round up when it comes to people) are actively looking for work. What the unemployment rate fails to consider are the folks who have given up looking and those folks who have settled for something temporary or part-time. A more accurate number would be around fifteen percent of United States population.

I paint this economical portrait for two reasons: first, to persuade you that I do indeed know my shit, and second, to convince myself that it is not entirely my fault that I couldn't land a job selling lattes to yuppies if I tried.

I graduated in the midst of what I have described as a recession. I had entered the job market during the worst time my generation has ever gone through. Things were going smoothly in the nineties and into the new millennium, or as Will Smith rapped, the "Willenium." Graduate students were salivating at the thought of their big paychecks.

Then, in 2001 the tech sector blew up, creating a surplus of available people. Then there were these crazy self-righteous motherfuckers who crashed some big ass planes into the New York skyline, killing themselves and thousands of innocent people. Not only did this horrible act take the lives of thousands of innocent people, it affected the airlines, the stock market, and everyone's perceptions of security.

Then corporate scandals began to unfold with the shady reporting of Enron and WorldCom. The debacles, as everyone likes to call them, told us that we really shouldn't trust large corporations. That seed of mistrust, planted in the minds of currency holders, resulted in reluctant investors. Without money, companies cannot grow. With no growth, there are no new jobs. With no new jobs, there is no spending. With no spending, there is no need for production. You get the point.

The SARS epidemic came along a while later, scaring the shit out of us and further exacerbating the predicament of the travel and international trade industries. As if international trade wasn't bad enough, the threat of a new fatal disease scared people from traveling between countries.

All of these events created quite a unique wrinkle in time not in favor of the job seeker.

I found myself entering into the American economy in 2003. I witnessed businesses kick the shit out of competitors. As much as I have described the ills of Wal-Mart and Starbucks, I would lie if I claimed that I didn't patronize either of those establishments. I love the convenience and the prices at Wal-Mart, and I find Starbucks coffee to be hundreds of times better than many other coffee shops. Businesses are extremely cost conscience. They continually seek out ways to increase market share, profit share, and reduce costs. As companies employ more and more measures to remain competitive, life becomes more and more dismal for the job seeker.

BIDNESS SKOOL

I was traveling around Mexico for work when I made the decision to get my MBA. I knew that I would be working down there for another year and I wanted to start graduate school directly after I returned, therefore I had to organize everything via email. I did all of my research from Internet cafés in remote locations like San Cristobol, Chiapas, and Oaxaca. Reasonably, many of the top business schools require very high GMAT scores, an undergraduate business degree, high undergraduate grades, strong letters of recommendation, and two years of professional work experience. Unfortunately, as an anthropology major with no prior business experience I didn't satisfy most of those requirements.

Also, the costs for top tier institutions were incredibly high, at around fifty grand in tuition alone, and my work in Mexico wasn't going to provide me with much cash. Because I was still considered a resident of Texas, I began researching local schools for the in-state tuition. I found that the University of Texas at El Paso, the University of Texas at San Antonio, and Texas A&M International University all had more flexible entrance requirements that I could satisfy and seemed relatively affordable. While still in Mexico, I applied to each of them, and, to my surprise, was accepted to all three.

Of the three schools, Texas A&M International was a fairly new university and offered me a tuition break and a paid assistantship. It was located in the city of Laredo, which lies just across the Rio Grande from Mexico and is well known for its heavy rail and truck traffic, due in part to the North American Free Trade Agreement, also known as NAFTA. Since 1994, trade between the U.S. and Mexico has been facilitated by NAFTA, which enabled non-tariff trade. The United States can freely ship goods to Mexico for assembly and Mexico can ship the assembled goods back. The long-term effects of NAFTA are still unclear, but traffic is heavy in Laredo and the borderlands are now scattered with *maquiladoras*, cheap labor factories. I love Mexico almost as much as I love the states and thought that I would be interested in studying international trade, so I accepted their offer. It seemed like the perfect opportunity.

Unfortunately, it wasn't. I knew that the school was new and sought to increase enrollment by giving tuition breaks, but I didn't realize that they did this for as many people as possible. It seemed like every foreign and out of state student had received a tuition break. Many of the students, my classmates, were from developing countries and the cheap tuition was their ticket to an American education. A classmate from Cypress indicated that because the institution was in the United States, people back home would assume it was a good school. They also had a very young and inexperienced faculty. Most of my professors, with a few exceptions, were bad, really bad. They had earned their degrees from places not particularly well known for cranking out business professors and would teach class with manufactured PowerPoint slide shows. As soon as I entered that school, I realized I had to transfer to someplace better.

The city itself emulated the mindset of the university; it was unchallenging and not at all intellectually stimulating. Laredo, a dusty pathway between two giants in the international trade game, had seen no pretty days. It was like an island community separated by hundreds of miles from the two nearest cities, San Antonio, Texas and Monterrey, Mexico. The city lacked the businesses and the resources that typify other cities. It was hot as fuck and there were virtually no trees and absolutely no water. There were no communal areas for people to spend time. There were no bookstores, no coffee houses, and no parks. What existed was a city whose only purpose was to function for trade. There was a depressed downtown, whose brick buildings housed stores with cheap junk produced at the *maquiladoras*. The growth was haphazard and pointed north, like a baby's arm extending to its mother. Northbound Interstate 35 was scattered with apartment complexes and chain restaurants. The only successful businesses in Laredo are chains, as the citizens reject anything outside of their mediocre, predictable, routines. Laredo was ranked as the worst city in the United States, according to a comparative study[1] and its "bustle, lack of intellectual stimulation, poverty, high crime rate, and heat will try anyone's patience."

Armed with a little business school experience, thanks to Texas A&M, I applied and was accepted to Southwest Texas State University, located a few hours drive north, between San Antonio and Austin. I spent the next two years there. It wasn't a great school but it was a million times better than that Laredo bullshit. For the most part, the professors were bright, passionate, and held high expectations. The students were a hundred steps above the Laredo crowd too.

Business schools try to simulate real life work environments. Because most working environments utilize teams, MBA programs include plenty of group projects. At Southwest, my groups were often difficult to manage due to conflicting outside schedules. Invariably, what should have been regular meetings and discussions morphed into a division of specialty and a last minute assembly of papers and presentations. This, I guess, is not that far from what happens in many work environments after all. Although the school was leaps and bounds over Texas A&M International, it was still

---

1.　"Book Ranks Laredo Worst City to Live in" by Celina Alverado, *Laredo Morning Times*, Wednesday, March 31, 2004.

shadowed by institutions like the University of Texas at Austin. Then again there was a $40,000 difference in tuition and I feel I got my money's worth.

ENTREPRENEURS

My MBA program was catered toward working adults, therefore the majority of the classes were held in the evening. Most of the students held full-time jobs during the day and completed the program in three years by going part-time. On the other hand, I was more interested in finishing the program as soon as possible. I always figured that it would be more beneficial to have the degree and then accept a higher paying position. This cost/benefit analysis seemed straightforward; if I went to school part-time and delayed my graduation, it could have cost me an entire year of MBA level income. But more to the point, I wanted to enjoy my days while I still had them. I enjoyed waking up late and leisurely sipping coffee on my patio while reading *Financial Times*.

Because my undergraduate degree was in anthropology, I was required to take a number of undergraduate business courses before I could officially pursue my MBA. Conveniently, many of these were offered during the daytime and I took as many as I could handle. One of the first was *Studies in Entrepreneurship*, and it remains one of the best classes I have ever taken.

The class met twice a week. One of the days was always reserved for successful entrepreneurs to come in and speak about their own experiences. Business owners would speak about their personal backgrounds and their trials and tribulations as entrepreneurs. The second meeting was reserved to work on the business and class discussions. Individual teams were assigned to complete business plans from the ground up and then present them to venture capitalists. Dr. Bell led the class.

Early in the semester we were encouraged to think of business ideas to pitch to the rest of the class to formulate teams. I pitched an idea for an import and retail company because I'd always wanted to incorporate my passion for travel and cultural studies with business. My company would import artisan goods from Latin America and sells them in other markets for a profit. I explained that the key to the success of this particular company would be to create a niche market that celebrated the artists and their respective cultures. Recent trends indicated that consumers desired artisan goods, and from a general analysis it seemed that there weren't any retailers that also informed the consumers about the goods, at least no branded businesses. There are retailers such as World Imports and Pier One Imports that appeal to yuppies, but they did not offer details of the product history and did not ensure fair trade. When someone buys a wooden devil mask from my business, for example, it will give them the experience of being in that village buying the art from the artist directly. My business will eliminate the disconnect from producer to consumer.

Others in the class presented a buffet of ideas, including a sea-food restaurant, a t-shirt company, a burrito stand, and a chair manufacturer. After the few idea men spoke, the remainder of the class gravitated to the companies they were interested in working for. A graduate student and a handful of undergraduates joined my team. I told them that I expected the project to be the best in the class and that we'd possibly have a solid business that would be suitable to launch. As the one with the business idea, the group looked to me for mentoring and motivation.

We held our initial meeting and brainstorming session at a coffee house so that we could all get to know each other and figure out everybody's strong points. The team was then divided into basic areas of specialization for initial research and information gathering. There were team members responsible for financial information and projections, marketing, competitive analysis, survey design and analysis, and business writing. In addition to my role as project manager, I was responsible for researching the existing companies similar to the one we were creating.

The team started out strong but quickly deteriorated. After our first meeting, we agreed to a timeline for specific tasks that the team members were to complete, and nobody completed a single thing. The little that was accomplished was half-ass and inconclusive. Frustrated, I immediately organized another meeting to ensure that we were all of a collective mindset regarding what needed to be done and when. One positive aspect of a professional work environment is that employers can fire unproductive employees at will, and I would have loved to fire those slackers. However, in this situation all my team could do was allocate a lower amount of points to the low and non-performing members.

At our next meeting, I asked my team to explain their progress and to show me what they had completed. Again, those slackers either didn't complete the work at all or presented crap. I was furious. I quickly realized that these students hadn't signed on with my idea because they were smart or dedicated; rather they gravitated to me after my presentation because they intuitively knew that I would carry the workload. They figured that because I wanted the work to be solid, I would hold their undergraduate hands while we completed the assignment. It was then that I realized that I was dealing with people that had to be told what to do rather than people that enjoy the empowerment of decision-making. Beyond project management, I had an additional role as a micromanaging hand holder, actually having to tell college seniors what to do and how to do it.

I hated working with that group. I couldn't handle half-ass work any longer and I was not about to compromise the integrity of the project. I spoke with Dr. Bell, and with his permission I was able to kick the weakest performer off my team. The guy had done nothing all semester, just wanting to barely pass the class so he could go on to a mediocre job where they don't require intellect and drive, at some place that employed mediocre dorks.

Once he was booted out, the rest of the group showed considerable improvement. The work they supplied was never as complete as it should have been, but it was okay. Together with the other graduate student on my team, Chad, I had to compile the mediocre work from the undergraduates and repair and revise. Chad and I had to redo practically everything they did because they made mistakes that would get the business killed in its launch. Like the bidness skool axiom "garbage in, garbage out," if the information inputted is erroneous, the results will be worthless. By the end of the semester we had a business plan that I was proud of. The finished project was a business plan describing a company called "World Artisans." It was a business that would allow Chad and I to travel all over the world with our cameras and wallets, the perfect mix of business and pleasure.

Although frustrating at times, working in that team was an exceptional experience. I learned more about group dynamics, motivation and leadership than in any other position I have ever held. Ironically, this was mainly due to those under performing undergraduates.

Besides creating a business plan, I learned an extraordinary amount about entrepreneurs. Throughout the semester there were about fifteen business owners who told their story to our class. They were from all kinds of different backgrounds, had different goals, and were in a variety of industries. The CEOs that spoke my semester owned and operated real estate agencies, magazines, bus lines, restaurants, oil refineries, art galleries, and consulting firms.

All entrepreneurs share certain similar characteristics. They are not risk averse. They surround themselves with people that are smarter than they are. They are dedicated and willing to spend a crazy amount of time building and operating their businesses. An entrepreneur knows that any business has only two possible scenarios: failure and success. Failure means personal capital can be permanently lost, as well as credibility, therefore entrepreneurs must be willing to take chances. Those seeking a dependable outcome without personal capital on the line do not make good entrepreneurs.

Entrepreneurs surround themselves with the brightest people they can find. Any company can succeed at one point and then later fail for lack of innovation and of lack of competitive leverage. Entrepreneurs may have raw ideas that need to be fine-tuned, tested, and implemented. Rarely can one person assume all of the responsibilities; therefore they must have good people working with them to strategically give them advantages.

Entrepreneurs work more hours than anybody. The owners are responsible for ensuring the success of the organization; therefore they must spend as much time as it takes to get the job done. Additionally, entrepreneurs must be dynamic. The business realm is constantly changing. Technology is constantly innovating. Regulations are constantly altering. Market forces change. Consumer demands change. Supplier prices change. Supply chain operations change. An entrepreneur has to not only be able to adapt to the changing environment, but must anticipate it. Think about all of the companies that were once the shit but are now gone. I am revealing my age by this, but I remember a clothing label called Cross Colors. Cross Colors was the shit in the early nineties. They hopped on the urban hip-hop music street trends. All of their clothes were brightly colored and baggy. They were huge bright orange jeans and huge purple shirts. I haven't seen anyone wearing Cross Colors since about

1991. Because Cross Colors didn't foresee change and adapt beyond a short-term fad, they were eliminated.

Some people become entrepreneurs because they simply have the drive and passion for self-employment and risk. Some people really don't have a choice but to become entrepreneurs; they are broke as fuck and invent ways to keep afloat.

Walk the main streets of Tijuana as soon as you cross into the Mexican border. As you do, you will be bum-rushed by pharmacists, people who want to introduce you to pharmacists, prostitutes, people who want to take you to prostitutes, people who want to show you where all of the hot spots are, children selling you Chiclets, men playing the accordion, street vendors selling black market CDs, and men charging for you to have your picture taken next to a donkey spray painted with zebra stripes. These are all poor people who became entrepreneurs out of necessity. In an absence of jobs and the capital to begin solid businesses, people often strive to satisfy a demand or create a demand and then satisfy it.

My brother Brian and I once rented a car in San Diego for a trip down the beautiful peninsula of Baja California, Mexico. Although well traveled in the rest of the country, at the time neither of us knew anything about the peninsula, which contributed to our excitement. As we drove southbound on the highway through the dessert, we realized one thing: there were hardly any gas stations. We passed one station when our tank was over a quarter full, but then continued to drive a hundred miles without passing another. Soon we were approaching an empty tank and, according our rudimentary map, it appeared that the next town, Catavina, was about forty miles away. Instead of turning around and trying to make it back a hundred miles, we decided continue trekking south and hoped that Catavina would have fuel. Due to the conditions of the road and its meandering path through the mountains (not clearly evident on our map), it took us about an hour and a half to travel those forty miles and we rolled in to Catavina on fumes. It turned out that the town wasn't a town at all, just a single hotel and a gas station. It also turned out that the gas station hadn't been a functioning gas station in many, many years. We were screwed.

Siphon Man, as we accurately dubbed him, saved our lives, or at least our vacation. He was a local entrepreneur that had decided to capitalize on the "unprepared Gringo tourist" market. He would drive his pick-up to a nearby gas station and fill huge metal barrels of fuel to carry up and down the highway looking for situations like ours. Hours after helplessly waiting for a miracle in Catavina, he came down the road and used a homemade siphon hose to fill our tank, for a hefty fee. At over three times the market cost it was the most expensive gas in the world, and was probably mixed with a bit of water and sand to stretch his buck, but it was exactly what we needed. The best entrepreneurs find a need to satisfy.

Sometimes entrepreneurs aren't that successful. During another trip to Mexico, Brian and I were sipping coffee at a café in the town center of Oaxaca City. Oaxaca is a beautiful city that attracts a lot of travelers. Wherever there are lots of poor locals and relatively wealthy tourists, the locals will try to sell stuff. Among the shoe shines, Chiclets, bracelets, and hammocks, we witnessed the efforts of the "Drunk Bandito," another breed of entrepreneur. The Drunk Bandito, a seemingly intoxicated Mexican dressed in an old revolutionary costume with a waxed moustache, would approach tourists in the sidewalk cafés and pretend to shoot them with a fake gun. He would then hold his hand out for a tip, presumably for his entertainment value. I gave him some money because I appreciated the absurdity of the situation, but most others weren't interested.

As I mentioned earlier with Cuba, occasionally people will set up their own businesses with their own rules in the black market. Prostitution, cigars, and even personal apartment rentals are huge business in Cuba.

The same thing has happened throughout the United States, notably with ethnic minorities who have always had to get in where they fit. If environmental pressures, including lack of resources and rejection, from the ruling majority exists then people must find their niches. Inner cities are notoriously depressed and most do not have the vitality that other communities have. The people are broke and there are no jobs, unless they want to take a job that would keep them impoverished such as a minimum wage job at a fast food chain. Therefore these neighborhoods experience an emergence of entrepreneurial drug dealers, pimps, rappers, and athletes to name a few. Legal or not, ethical or not, economic forces push people to survival and money is to be made, it's just too bad when it has to be for crack or ass.

Russell Simmons was on the cover of a recent *Business Week*[1] calling him the "CEO of Hip Hop." The article painted a picture of Mr. Simmons as a mogul. Along with partner Rick Rubin, he started Def Jam records and was responsible for putting rap music on the map. Some of the first rap artists signed by Def Jam were the Beastie Boys and Run DMC—two very innovative groups of rappers who brought the inner-city sound to the masses by introducing rock guitar riffs in the lyrics. He owns an urban clothing line called Phat Fashions. Phat, of course, means hip, beautiful, and cool. Like a hip-hop Gap, Phat Fashions contains such clothing lines as: Phat Farm Men's Wear, Baby Phat, Phat Farm Boys, Baby Phat Girlz, Phat Farm Footwear, Accessories, and Run Athletic (named after Run from Run DMC). Under the Def Jam name, he started the popular Def Comedy Jam, then the Def Poetry Jam, and Russell Simmons' Def Poetry Jam on Broadway, all featuring prominent black and non-black comedians and poets.

---

1.   "The CEO of Hip Hop" by Susan Berfield, *Business Week*, October 27, 2003

Simmons has created a pre-pay debit card aimed specifically for those who don't have bank accounts. He has developed a soda manufactured by Pepsi called DefCon 3. He produced the *Nutty Professor* movie. He is also known as an urban expert, providing consulting services to companies, such as Motorola and Courvoisier, who want to target the youthful, hip-hop market. Motorola recognized that the cellular phone is as much a fashion accessory as it is functional; they consult with Simmons because street trends start in the streets. Courvoisier had been mentioned in rap lyrics for years. High status rappers, such as Busta Rhymes, openly rap about drinking Courvoisier. The year that Busta's "Pass the Courvoisier" was released, Courvoisier's sales increased twenty percent. Simmons, like many urban entrepreneurs, began as a hustler, sometimes selling drugs in Queens, New York.

Niggaz With Attitude, or NWA, was a rap group that popularized the gangsta style of rap that exploded in California in the late '80s and early '90s. The group included Dr. Dre, who would go on to become an entrepreneur himself and start his own record label, Death Row. Death Row would go on to produce some of the biggest and most money generating rappers ever, including two that even my parents are familiar with: Snoop Doggy Dogg and Eminem. NWA also included Ice Cube, who would eventually go solo and produce the most politically-charged series of phenomenal records of the genre: *Amerikkka's Most Wanted*, *Lethal Injection*, and *The Predator*. Ice Cube would go on to become an entrepreneur and produce and star in films such as *Friday*. In addition to the prolific and influential careers of its members, NWA was responsible for many things. They brought attention to California's ghettos and they initiated fear within mainstream America by representing a collective mindset that said, "Fuck the police." Entrepreneurial member Eazy E, who got the capital from dealing drugs, financed the group. This model has been repeated by modern rappers like Jay Z, who used to sell crack, and 50 Cent, who boasts about being shot nine times.

Historically, immigrants have always been restricted to their own communities and have been forced to become entrepreneurs. During the great immigrations to America, immigrants seeking the American dream and to get a piece of the democratic entrepreneurial pie would arrive in large port cities like New York. Influxes of Irish and Asians filled the New York City. When they arrived they were confronted with problems of racism and exclusion and were forced to live in ethnic enclaves.

In New York, Asians were denied employment in many sectors and thus began a trend of entrepreneurship. They specialized in laundry and dry cleaning services and set up shop with these types of businesses. Over time, Asian entrepreneurs have shifted their focus. They discovered that Americans love to eat. Although still offering laundry and dry cleaning services, they now own restaurants. Americans may not hire them, but they sure will eat their cooking.

My brother Brian was an entrepreneur in the early '90s during the techno music rave era. He realized that he loved the environment and wanted to capitalize on the culture, so he opened a trendy "smart bar" service. The smart bar was an extralegal enterprise that served smart drinks, essentially Tang smoothies, to thirsty raver kids. As raves were underground parties typically held in empty warehouses, sometimes outside of the law, there were never any drinks available for the thirsty partiers. Brian partied and served two-dollar cups of iced Tang to pay his rent in college and fund his trips to the Dallas party scene.

Everybody is an entrepreneur to some degree, depending on the degree of risk and capital invested. Even the folks that play it safe and open franchise stores in proven chains are entrepreneurs. I respect those who create and operate their own businesses out of passion and drive. They put their own asses on the line, their own capital, and all of their time. There is a tremendous learning curve associated with becoming an entrepreneur. Rarely does an entrepreneur succeed at the first try. You learn the most from failure. One must fail and struggle in order to avoid similar situations in the future.

During my months of constant rejection, I thought that I would be forced into a culture of entrepreneurs. I would have to take the World Artisan business plan to the bank, or think of something else to do.

It was just a matter of time before I set up my own lemonade stand.

THE FEDS

I began my job search in March after returning from spring break in South Padre Island (which is the bomb by the way; it's like Mardi Gras on the beach). Because my professional experience was limited, I decided to explore general areas that interested me such as international economics, market research, diplomacy, math modeling, analysis work, and teaching. I figured that even without work experience, the MBA had enough weight to land me a decent job.

My first choice was the governmental sector because I was attracted to the non-volatile nature of the work and wanted to be involved in some cool international shit. I discovered that all government openings were now posted to a central Internet job board, appropriately called usajobs.com. Like monster.com or any of the other Internet employment brokers, the site allows one to complete a résumé and additional information to facilitate the application process. That seemed efficient, but once I targeted positions that I was actually interested in, the process went from seemingly easy and time efficient to the most time-consuming antiquated system I have ever seen.

From certain agencies and categories, I targeted positions like "Intelligence Research Analyst", and "Budget Analyst". I had to fight through the verbiage jungle of each of descriptions, which made applying far from easy. All of the positions that I wanted had very specific instructions on how to go about completing the application. Usually, I had to fax all of my school transcripts, along with a specifically designed résumé reflecting the job code and all contact names and numbers of past employers and references. That wouldn't have been a big deal except that my education began at a community college, then transferred to a university with a semester abroad, and finished with graduate school at two different institutions. That amounted to five transcripts per application. Most of the positions also required that an essay or written responses addressing lengthy criteria be faxed along with the transcripts and résumé. I couldn't help thinking that with all this faxing and the specific application processes for each position, what the hell was the point of the centralized job board? I have nothing against agencies trying to ensure they have the best fit for each position, but fuck, that shit is ridiculous.

Government agencies usually had only one position available and that position would be filled in the next six to nine months. That position, which required an essay, faxed transcripts, and a tailored résumé, gave priority to current federal employees. That meant that it was not likely I was going to ever gain employment with the government.

I spent about a month searching governmental jobs and faxing all of the shit they demanded, only to receive letters weeks or even months afterwards indicating that I was not selected for the positions. If that ridiculous red tape, bureaucratic, time consuming, antiquated shit is any illustration of how the governmental sector actually is, then fuck working for the government. Why is that shit so terribly organized that a million bureaucrats have to look at a piece of paper before it can be processed?

Not all governmental sectors hire in the same bullshit way, but then again not all white dudes are dorks.

I did manage to go through the first phase of the Foreign Service interview process. The Foreign Service is the agency that places Americans throughout the world as they protect American business involvement. This sounded like the bomb; being an American diplomat around the globe. It sounded like an excellent fit with my interests and background.

Understandably, the selection process for the Foreign Service is difficult. First, I had to complete an online résumé and answer a series of questions. I was told that if the Department of State felt that I qualified for the next step, they would arrange for me to complete the next phase of the application process, a written exam. I guess my interest in foreign policy, experiences abroad, and my MBA earned me a spot at the test-taking center.

The test was set up like many other standardized tests. There was an essay section, where I was to select one of the two topics presented and write a persuasive essay, and a multiple choice section dealing with U.S. history and foreign policy. I prepped as much as I did for my GMAT, which isn't saying a whole lot. The exam was at eight, and I wasn't able to get a lot of sleep the night before because I had been in the routine of staying up late for night school. I sat at the small desk and opened the paper with the eraser end of my pencil, just like I did for the standardized exams in high school. The two essay topics were: should the government flip the bill for art and should there be standardized testing for schools.

I wrote about how I felt standardized tests should be used, but to a degree. My arguments were that, if the tests were not used in conjunction with other measures, teachers could potentially not teach anything other than test preparation material, and that could water down the educational process. Overall, I felt I did well on the exam, although not superbly on the writing portion. I received a letter in July stating that my scores weren't high enough to be considered for the next phase. I was one of the seventy-five percent who didn't make the cut. Ironically, it was standardized testing that failed to correctly assess my capabilities and knowledge.

I also found out that the Department of Labor offered a program that they just began a year earlier. It was specifically designed for

MBAs, putting fresh graduates to work in different departments within the organization. The program had mentors in each department and helped identify through practice where the new employee had the best fit. These types of programs allow graduates to gain exposure to numerous departments and pinpoint their areas of specialty. At the same time, the employers gain better workers with deeper knowledge and understanding of company operations. Like most governmental sectors, the Department of Labor was no different in regards to the application process. They required a specifically tailored résumé, all of my transcripts, letters of recommendation, and an essay. My essay turned out to be ten pages long discussing my areas of expertise.

What bothered me was that the Department of Labor asked the applicants to write about examples of team leading, motivation, project involvement, and so on. What a huge waste of time; only MBAs were applying! We all have those experiences. The first year the Department of Labor offered the program a little over one hundred MBA graduates applied for the seventeen positions. In 2003, there were over four hundred and fifty MBA graduates competing for the same seventeen openings. A month or so went by and I didn't get a call. In fact, I called them to ask about where I was in the process and they told me that all of the applicants that were being considered had already been contacted.

TURNING JAPANESE
(or trying to)

In case we didn't find jobs right away, my girlfriend and I had a back-up plan. Long before graduation, we had applied to the Japanese Embassy to teach English in Japan for a year. Advertisements for these positions are quite common at colleges, and from what I knew of these organizations, the Japanese Embassy was the highest paying and most credible. I knew a handful of folks that did the work after college or graduate school, and they all loved it.

We found that the Japanese government is a lot like ours: a million people had to look at our applications before getting approval. The Japanese Embassy Teaching program (JET) runs on the same bullshit antiquated systems that the usajobs.com site does. You cannot send a résumé or even fax the information; you have to mail it directly to the Washington, DC office. To qualify for the JET program, applicants need to fulfill only two requirements: have a four-year degree, and be available for the next year. The application is cumbersome. It must be downloaded as a PDF file and actually be typed, as in with a typewriter (who the fuck has a typewriter anymore). Luckily, my girlfriend worked at a company that still had a typewriter available. We dusted it off and stayed at her office after hours for several nights completing those twenty-something pages of application.

I have a college degree. I speak Spanish and have studied German and French. I have lived in and traveled to numerous states and countries. I have teaching experience as a mentor and a tutor. I have worked with an international clientele in the tourist industry for over two years. And finally, I have an MBA. I thought that I was the fucking bomb for the position and I more than satisfied the only two requirements. I had three letters of recommendation typed from professors and employers stating that I had excellent skills. Dr. Bell wrote an impressive letter where he described me as being in the top ninety-five percentile of all the students he had ever taught, including doctoral candidates. I had copies of all my university transcripts, except for the semester I spent abroad but it was only one semester and the coursework was reflected in my university transcript. Everything was ready. Everything had been checked and double-checked for completion. Everything was copied three times, as requested by the Japanese Consulate. My girlfriend and I mailed our application packages together and awaited the responses, which were to come in the next months. The packages were delivered by December 2002. Interviews were to take place by March and decisions were to be made by May.

In March, Breanna received an invitation to be interviewed in person at the Houston office. A few days later, I received a card in the mail that indicated that my application package was incomplete and that I would not be considered further. Incomplete and not considered! Furiously, I called them immediately and got machine after machine. I couldn't believe that they would fail to consider me because of the grades for the semester I spent in Mexico, as part of my *undergraduate* degree, had not been reflected in my package. Bastards.

I have a graduate degree that I completed with an A average. My undergraduate grades were also very high. I did one semester abroad in Mexico and was waiting on an official transcript from the Mexican University. Not that it was very relevant to the position, but anyone looking at the transcripts I provided could make inferences of the study abroad grades. It stated in my university transcript that coursework only transfers if the grade is at least a C. I was once again the victim of a rigid bureaucracy. I called the interviewer at the Houston office and spoke with the person that would be interviewing my girlfriend.

"We applied as a couple. If we both cannot have the opportunity than neither of us would like to go."

I explained the absurdity of this situation and that I was obviously qualified for the position. Surprisingly enough, the interviewer seemed receptive to my concerns and placed a call to the Japanese representatives in Washington, DC. A few minutes later she called to inform me that they would not budge on their position. The really messed up thing is that, by the time this all went down I had actually received from Mexico the piece of paper that reflected the five classes in Mexican history and Spanish. "Can I fax them immediately," I begged. The answer was an insincere and automated "No, all material must be in by December 5th."

I didn't want to work for their rigid asses anyway.

WORKING THE NETWORK

Networking is essential for putting the lock down on a job. Eighty percent of all jobs are not advertised. Therefore, all of the postings on monster.com and other boards represent only a small portion of all open positions. Finding out about the other eighty percent can often require having the right connections. These need to be made as early as possible. Most of us are familiar with the tired old phrase "it's not what you know, but who you know."

I remembered a marketing professor talking about that in my second semester of graduate school. "Have lunches all the time with each other…get business cards…use friends and colleagues to find their connections," he would remind us. He was right. He just wasn't compelling enough for me to actually do it. I didn't have any money for lunches, and I wasn't going to finish school for another two years. Besides, if in the strange event that I could not find work, I would simply get a job at my brother's consulting company. Brian always assured me that there would be opportunities there, except, of course, when I actually needed one.

When I finished school, I had a really crappy network. Everyone I knew was like me: young and looking for a job. Then again, they were also very much unlike me in the respect that I was the only one in my circle with an advanced degree and a pursuit in business. Months before I graduated with my MBA, I notified everyone that I knew that I was looking for a position and that I could use all the help I could get. I made a few calls to friends and asked them for any leads and to keep an eye open for me. I sent emails to everyone I knew, asking the same from them. Either there were no leads at all, or the leads dried up.

Due to my background and personality, my network of friends consisted of a variety of different folks in various stages of their careers. I was friends with a few thirty-something musicians that made electronic music and sold jewelry on eBay, a thirty-year old architectural school dropout who had been unemployed for a year, a long-term friend who vaguely worked "with computers" (I still don't know what the hell that dude does, don't we all work with computers?), a social worker who flew all over the country to speak with tragedy victims, an ex-girlfriend who owned of a small school, a married couple that were developing a multimedia firm contributing to video games, a film editor, a manager of a logistics firm, a funds distributor for the United Way, an art teacher, and my brother Brian, the marketing researcher and part-time psychology professor.

Although an interesting mix of people and great in their own rights, it wasn't necessarily a strong business network. Most of the people listed were in their first position, playing the default game by accepting something within easy reach and abandoning prior goals, unemployed, underemployed, or only connected with those in the same community. They were an interesting bunch of folks and advanced in their respective fields, just no help to me.

After graduating and having absolutely no money and no prospects of having any money, I moved in with my girlfriend and her mother. She was kind enough to allow me to live in her country house temporarily for a hundred dollars rent, which I could still barely afford. There was no Internet in the house and because the house was in the outskirts of Austin, my cellular phone service was horrible. I had to make and receive calls by standing in the street.

Fortunately for me, the competitive business environment around Austin pushed local coffee shops to entice consumers. Some competed successfully by having a free wireless Internet service, as well as bottomless coffee cups.

All I had to do was make a one-time investment of fifty bucks to get the wireless card for my notebook computer and pay a daily two fifty for a bottomless coffee. Making such small investments, I spent my entire summer at the nicest coffee house like it was my own private living room. In the mornings I would grab my computer and leave the house for my daily job search, only to return in the evening.

Breanna's younger sister, Leann, worked in the hills of Austin at a country club for the "rich white folk," as I like to call them. She served food on a weekly basis at a professional networking meeting. She recommended to the two of us that we check it out, and she furnished us with the email address of the president. I emailed this guy and stated my concerns and, although the structure was geared more to client references, he invited me to attend a meeting.

That Wednesday, Breanna and I arrived at that stuffy country club. I wore my best suit and was armed with a ton of résumés and business cards ready for some serious hand shaking and hobnobbing with the rich white folks. We showed up at eight and approached the desk where I was greeted by an overly cheerful woman who gladly took a twenty-dollar fee and handed me a nametag. The meeting was in a huge conference room and the tables were arranged in the shape of the letter U. I sat at an available seat while good strong coffee and a crappy breakfast, consisting of flour tortillas and scrambled eggs, were served.

The president welcomed everyone and explained the structure of the meeting for those of us that were new. We were to go around the room from one side to the other and introduce ourselves and describe our interests. Then, we were to provide and receive referrals. If they could be of any assistance, members would write on a little note card their name or the name of someone they know. Then there would be a showcasing where a member speaks for a while describing their business in some detail. Finally, we were all to go around the room again and say something that we liked about the networking meeting.

The person on the far right stood up and began the meeting.

"Hi my name is (whoever) and I represent (some company). (Repeat company slogan). The perfect referral for me today is (blah, blah, blah)."

I quickly noticed that everyone was following a specific format. Each person stood up, cheerfully introduced themselves, followed their introduction with a jingle, and finally ended it describing their client. They all spoke with the same dorky conformity that you would expect to hear from a Wal-Mart greeter. A dude working for a flashlight company would have stood and said, with a great big goofy smile, "Hi my name is Mark, and with us you will always see in the dark. The perfect referral for me is someone without electricity, or who lives outdoors," I imagined.

I was suspicious of their cheerfulness. How can these people really be happy when they have to stand up wearing their company logo golf knits and recite that informal automated shit? I imagined all of them wearing masks, actually hiding an internal struggle. I became sad for a moment as I watched this display of desperate networking. I thought of the scene in the movie *American Beauty* where the character of the wife spends her morning crying her eyes out and trying to psyche herself up for her shitty real estate job.

I noticed two things as the members stood and explained themselves. First, nobody was unemployed, and second, none of the companies or positions that these people had was the least bit interesting. They were all basically salespeople for mediocre companies.

My turn came along. "My name is Jon. I just finished graduate school. I am skilled in analysis, and fluent in Spanish. I am here to make networking connections so that I can find a job."

When the thirty or so members were finished with their song and dance routine it was referral time. Everyone tried to be of assistance by passing these note cards to different people. In the ten-minute period, I had received a grand total of two referrals from the thirty members. I looked at the cards that were passed to me and I read the messages. One was from a medical doctor who felt that I would be interested in an entrepreneurial opportunity; some bullshit "make your own hours and earn up to six figures" stupid shit. He later emailed me to describe it in greater ambiguity, saying that he had left his practice to pursue it. The second one was from a Mary Kay representative. The note suggested that I look into becoming one myself. The woman who handed me that card sat next to me and quietly explained that there are men who make a ton of money selling Mary Kay.

A set of emotions hit me. I was saddened by the utter lack of any useful connections. I was angered that I had woken up early, spent twenty dollars that I didn't have, and had attended that bullshit meeting. I was offended that the only referrals were to sling lipstick and to be my own boss.

After some dude spent fifteen minutes talking about whatever dumb shit he did we had to go around the room again, this time to generate feedback.

"I like the effectiveness of the meeting," someone said.

"I really liked learning about the different businesses and roles," someone else added.

When it came to my turn, I really wanted to respond in an irreverent way and tell these motherfuckers that they should tone down the dorky ass shit and find a way to attract a more diverse variety of professionals.

However, I bit my tongue.

"It was nice to have met all of you, and I appreciate the opportunity."

Breanna's one referral was from a bullshit modeling agency to either be a model or to be a scout for models. Dorks.

JOB FAIRS

All colleges have career fairs to help connect graduating students with hiring companies. Months before I graduated I went to one such fair at Southwest Texas State University. My school was a good school, but not a great school and that fact was reflected by the opportunities presented at the career fair. It seemed that all of the companies represented were local and they weren't even specifically targeting MBA students at all. There were a lot of local businesses in attendance, most of them looking for entry-level sales professionals or something of that nature. I remember not being impressed at all with the turnout.

Breanna received her first job offer and accepted it, as she had no idea when there would be another one. Her title would be financial analyst for a company based in San Antonio. Because I was broker than broke, paying bills by participating in pharmaceutical research studies, Breanna offered to support me to a while I was unemployed. We soon moved into a nice house in the center of the historical neighborhood, north of downtown San Antonio.

Once I was settled in San Antonio, I added browsing the local classified ads to my daily job search routine. From the paper, I learned that there was going to be a career fair at a local mall, which would include some of the large employers in the area, such as USAA and World Savings. I researched who was going to be present and prepared a stack of résumés and cover letters. There were a total of maybe five companies that I was remotely interested in talking to.

I arrived at the mall on the day of the career fair and noticed a ton of other people, all in suits carrying packets of résumés. Jesus, there were a shitload of motherfuckers in the same boat as me. Due to the sheer volume of folks trying to meet employers, I spent way too much of my time there just waiting in line. I would just hand my résumé to somebody if I could circumvent actually standing in line for an hour and then handing it to them. World Savings had the shortest line of any of the few businesses that interested me. I patiently waited in that line and then briefly spoke with the representatives. They told me that they would accept my résumé at the fair, but I should also visit their website and submit my résumé online.

A lot of the representatives said the same shit. "We are not accepting résumés here, but you can apply on our websites." I estimate that I was told that by nearly half of all the representatives at the career fair. If that was the case, then why the fuck were they at the mall that day wasting both of our time? It would have been easier to submit my résumé online instantly, from home in my pajamas instead of putting on a suit, driving to the mall, and waiting in lines. Besides, I had already submitted my information online anyway.

By far, the most popular employer at that career fair was USAA, an insurance company that services the military. Because there is such a huge military presence in San Antonio, they have a humongous facility there and tons of former military job seekers were attracted to them. Their display was so popular that it had the longest line; I mean a really fucking long line that apparently wasn't moving. The line extended way down the hallway to the mall's exit doors. I walked by that line several times hoping that it would get shorter. That never happened; in fact it actually grew longer. Wanting to save some time, I approached the representatives from USAA.

"I just want to drop off my résumé."

"That is what the line is for," they told me. I couldn't just simply place my résumé in the tub within arm's reach along with the ten thousand others.

I went all the way to the end of that long ass line and waited along with the other poor slobs. I waited in line for an hour, just to hand a piece of paper to someone. I started thinking about how the entire process was inefficient and they could have used my skills to organize that event. I finally met with a representative who was obviously not very eager to be there. She reminded me of a disgruntled cashier at a fast food chain or something communicating with her words the programmed phrase, "can I help you," but using nonverbal communication to indicate that she didn't want to help you at all. In fact she didn't even want to be there. I handed my résumé to this woman.

"We'll be in contact if there is a fit," she said with the same uninterested tone.

That was, by far, the worst job fair experience I have ever had.

I found out about the next career fair just in the nick of time. I was browsing the website for the business school at the University of Texas at Austin to determine if I could utilize any of their alumni services because I had finished my undergraduate degree there. While conducting my research, I noticed that there was a business fair that was going on that same day until five o'clock. I quickly got ready and drove to the Austin convention center.

I arrived in my black suit and bypassed the nametag stand. Instantly, I was amazed. Compared to the career fair held at Southwest Texas, there were tons of employers present, and they weren't crappy local ones, like the police department of some hick Texas town. They were impressive national and global finance, marketing, and business development companies. The students present at the fair were equally impressive. Unlike the crowd at the San Antonio mall, they were all were wearing suits and had their résumés in leather binders just like me. I started at the front of the convention center and made my way to as many representatives as possible before they packed up and left.

I met with representatives from many Fortune 500 companies that had exciting opportunities for graduating business students. None of these jobs were crappy sales positions. Instead, they were analyst, associate, and rotational positions. Each and every one of them sounded great and I was excited to actually learn that there were real companies out there looking for raw business talent.

I spoke with a representative from a consulting company who was looking to fill positions for financial analysis work. He explained that the financial analysis and statistical modeling would be used to estimate certain measures in litigation cases, such as time off from work and lost productivity. That's cool as fuck. Instead of lying and speaking with a fake passion, I was honestly excited about the majority of the companies that were present. "It pays to go to a good school," I thought as I remembered how shitty the other career fairs were. That $40,000 difference in tuition definitely had an impact. Not only did the one in Austin have great companies and great opportunities, it was a fair designed specifically for graduating business students. A glimmer of hope came over me as I met as many of the people and collected as many business cards as I could.

Most of the representatives admired my enthusiasm and my resourcefulness by attending the fair without being a business student at the University of Texas at Austin. However, one problem that I encountered by sneaking into the fair was that a lot of the companies were hiring only through business school career services that I was unable to use. Also, the career fair was intended for undergraduates in business, not MBAs. One representative told me that I might be overqualified for any positions that they were recruiting for and that I should attend the MBA fair scheduled for the following day. I had no idea such an event happening and became excited about the additional opportunities in store.

The next day, I snuck into the MBA career fair, which was very small, compared to the undergraduate one. I also encountered a bit of snobbery, with good reason. The MBA program at the University of Texas at Austin is a top tier program and to be accepted one must satisfy certain criteria: be a top performer as a BBA, have a couple of years of professional experience, score in the top percentile on the GMAT, and pay a shit load of money in tuition. I graduated from Austin as an undergrad; however my MBA was from Southwest Texas, a school with much more liberal entrance requirements. Representatives would politely accept my résumés and in turn, I asked for their business cards, but I knew that they were only interested in MBAs from UT Austin.

From the career fairs, I created a database of all of the connections that I had accumulated and emailed all of the people that I had met. They all got the same letter. "It was a pleasure meeting you…here is my résumé; please forward it to any interested departments." I sent out over a hundred emails like that. I either didn't get a response from them, or I got a form message stating that my résumé had been forwarded to the appropriate departments. I haven't heard anything more from any of them.

MARKETING MOJO

As a graduate of UT Austin, I did have access to their general job board. One day while job searching on my laptop from quite possibly one of the best coffee houses on the planet, the Spider House, I stumbled across an opening for a marketing internship that sounded pretty cool. The internship was for Mojo's Daily Grind, another kick-ass coffee house on the drag (hipster talk for the street adjacent to campus), and involved creating a marketing plan. I sent the dude an email explaining that I was a recent MBA graduate and would be interested in working on the project. That lazy ass, not atypical of coffee shop entrepreneurs I suspect, finally responded to me weeks later and wanted to get together with us for an interview.

I showed up and sat down at a table with the owner. Immediately, he put the sad fact of the job on the table: there would be no financial compensation. He then continued and admitted that he really had no business sense whatsoever. In fact, the internship posting was a cut and paste job, where he thought it just sounded cool. Although now less excited about the opportunity, I was still interested. Hell, it all goes on the résumé, right?

The owner went on about how other coffee shops are sprouting up all over the drag and that he has noticed some of his regulars were now going to the competition. Also, there was a noticeable decline in fresh college students patronizing coming in. I reluctantly agreed to accept the project. Reluctantly, because there was no pay and the owner's cooperation was questionable. After that first meeting I asked him to tell me everything he could about the business that might help me in my pursuits. That took about twenty minutes.

As with any project to strategically position a business, there is certain methodology that should be followed, otherwise the results may be unsubstantiated. I spent a ton of money to learn these basic steps in business school. I am sharing my own version of them here with you for a mere fifty bucks. I trust that you will have the check in the mail tomorrow.

1. **Know Yo' Shit:** To strengthen the position of a company, one must first become aware of the company's current position. It is important to know the philosophy, mission, objectives and goals of a business. It is important to know these because any solutions and ideas should be in alignment with the businesses core values.

2. **Tha 411:** Gather as much information as possible. This can be from primary sources such as conducting interviews, focus groups, administering questionnaires, and observation. It can also be gathered cheaper from secondary sources that have already done similar shit and have published results. Determining what type of information is needed varies by a few things: budget, time, and availability of secondary data.

3. **SWOT It Up, Yo**: Assess the Strengths, Weaknesses, Opportunities, and Threats (SWOT). This is done both internally and externally. A complete SWOT analysis will thoroughly assess direct and indirect competition, regulations, cost and timing technology, innovations, potential problems, ease of entry for competitors, and financial positioning.

4. **What Da Deal(z):** From SWOT Analysis problems, catastrophic or not, must be defined. They can be anything perti-

nent to the company and the industry. Examples include: shitty brand image, shitty positioning, wrong target market, inefficient processes, too much advertising, not enough philanthropy, management entrenchment, excessive debt leveraging, reduced market share, ease of entry for competitors, and so on.

5. **Pick One of Dem Bitches:** From the previous steps, a problem to address must be chosen. The chosen problem will be the one that needs immediate attention in terms of the environment and time.

6. **Solve & Implement Dat Shit:** Different problems have different solutions. One must first define the problem and then provide a series of possible solutions. After a series of logical solutions are created the best one should be chosen.

7. **Make F'Shizzle It Worked:** To determine if the solution is effective, one must perform the evaluation. Again, this is contingent on what the problem is and what the plan of action is. Problems in business are usually related to cost reductions and profit maximization. In the instance that the problem is a purely financial one, measurement is to record the financial positioning before and after implementation and on a trend basis.

For this particular project, the owner made it very clear to us that he was quintessentially broke and he had his hands full as the owner and manager of the business. He was also relatively opposed to change, as he liked his "fuck the big guys" platform and wanted to "keep it real" with his current cynical art crowd customers. These factors alone made for a less than ideal working relationship, one that I probably would have turned down if I had something better to do with my time. Change is a necessity for survival. Darwin taught us this in the 1800s. The same holds true for business.

The owner gave me what he considered pertinent information in my quest for a solid marketing plan; how he marketed in the past. However, there were no data as to how effective these marketing efforts were. Note to all of you reading this: data is very useful.

A couple of weeks later the owner and I had our second meeting. I discussed with him a series of possible problems and possible tracks for providing tentative solutions. A big concern of his was that many students were being turned off by the radical nature of his business. As a private business owner of a coffee shop, he had taken an oppositional stance against corporate giant Starbucks, which had moved into the drag a few years earlier. Consistent with this view, the matchbooks he had printed contained the slogan "Corporate Coffee Sucks." Also, a commissioned graffiti piece on the outside of his building contained the word "Corporate" with an X over it. Finally and more to the point, inside the shop hung a sign that appeared to have once read "Starbucks Coffee" but now subversively and quite cleverly contained the message "starFUCKs cOF-Fee." I love culture jamming.

I first wanted to determine if the atmosphere and the idea represented by this subversive coffee shop was indeed keeping people away. With no help from the owner or his subordinates, I designed a questionnaire, gathered a bunch of data, and analyzed the results. Interestingly enough, college students really didn't give a fuck about the coffee shop's image. The loss of clientele was due to other factors, like the seedy regulars that were always hanging out inside, scaring normal folks away. Not surprisingly, the decreased consumption was highly correlated with the onset of alternative hangouts.

In the end, I made a dozen recommendations to the owner regarding his marketing campaign. I determined what local publications that his clientele read to eliminate redundant costs. I also recommended that he try to partner with businesses and publications that shared similar philosophy.

A few months passed and my relationship with the owner of Mojo's deteriorated. Not only did he never help with the grunt aspects of the data collection, like distributing surveys, but also he never provided me with any feedback regarding the work. I can only imagine that he really had no clue of what a marketing plan entailed. Just so you all know, in the classical sense a marketing plan is a thorough analysis of the marketing landscape, with an end result of suggestions on how to make improvements. From the suggestions, the lead of the project decides to expend the resources to implement the suggestions. This dude just wanted free advertising; he expected me to do the actual implementation. At the end, I sent him a copy of the completed marketing plan and he mailed me a few letters of recommendation as I requested.

As far as I am aware, the marketing plan I developed was never implemented. Shortly after I had handed him my work, I noticed that he had posted another opening on the job board; seeking someone to implement a marketing plan.

MY FIRST BANK INTERVIEW

In Austin, there are a few research firms where any healthy eighteen to fifty-five year old can be used as a human guinea pig so that pharmaceutical companies can test new products before they are released on the market. Fellow UT alum, filmmaker Robert Rodriguez popularized this underground manner to make a quick lump sum. His legendary film debut *El Mariachi* was produced using the seven grand he earned from being a human test subject. To help myself subside during my months of unemployment, I participated in several such studies.

One Friday while I was in-house at a study facility, I received my very first callback from a potential employer. It was a bank and apparently I had submitted an application online for a "credit analyst" position. The hiring manager saw from my résumé that I had an MBA, and not wasting any time he told me the pay window and asked me if it would be acceptable. I agreed to the "high twenties to low thirties" range, even though far below what I was worth, as to not limit my options during a desperate time. I did tell him that any offer I'd consider would have to be on the higher end of that window. I mean come on; I had a master's degree in business.

We scheduled an interview for that following Monday and I prepared well. I knew the company, I looked very professional, and I brought along my portfolio. I sat in this guy's office as he described the position to me. It turned out that a credit analyst does little more than look at a few spreadsheets and report the findings to superiors. I asked about promotion potential, and he told me that it was a career tract for a banker, a salesman. After he gave a broad overview of the position he gave me some dumb scenario questions. Dumb because I feel that they weren't indicative of my decision-making capabilities or how I would handle certain specific job-related situations. I told the dude that to really give an appropriate response, I would have to know the role more. As the scenario related to superior-subordinate relationships, I would first have to know the boundaries and expectations of each. At the conclusion of the interview, I left him with several examples of statistical projects I had completed so he could see that I, an MBA graduate, indeed had the elementary spreadsheet expertise that the position required. It seemed fairly obvious that I was overqualified for the position.

Three months later, exactly three months later, I received a letter in the mail indicating that they had moved forward with another candidate. No shit. Here's a tip: either send a rejection letter sooner, like in a two week time frame, or don't send anything at all. The whole process seems problematic if it takes three months to send a rejection letter out, and it doesn't take a masters degree to realize that.

COUNTING MY CHICKENS IN PANAMA

Equipped with experience writing business plans, I was contacted by a company in San Antonio looking for someone to write a plan for them. Actually, the company was less like an actual company and more like one dude, an entrepreneur, and his part-time assistant. He had made his mark as an inventor of female niche products and now wanted to expand and needed the cold hard cash. Banks typically only make loans to businesses if there is a solid business plan that supports the financial success. He needed a business plan to take to the bank.

He interviewed me in a shared boardroom and told me of his products, and how he wanted to expand his operation. He had developed certain tool sets that were already for sale in a few stores, but wanted to get them distributed to more retail outlets. Basically, he just needed some supporting evidence and technical writing that would tell a loaning institution that his loan would be worthwhile. His idea was all about niche marketing. "Woman are shopping…woman are doing handyman work around the house…I want to see if there is a market for this list of products in these areas."

Writing the business plan paid three grand. I described my background and my specialty and he was confident that I would be able to complete the job. We shook on the deal and agreed that the project was mine.

At the same time, Breanna was offered the position in San Antonio. Things were looking up for the both of us and it had only been a couple of months since we graduated. She was to start work in just three weeks and of course wanted to make the best use of her remaining time without work. Because the American work structure only allows two weeks of vacation per year, we had to bounce. We celebrated our good fortune with a trip to Panama. It was Pantastic.

Panama was amazing. The beaches, the jungles, the people, the simplicity of life, the food, everything was awesome. Visiting the Third World, where life is different and simple and broke, really helps me to alleviate the woes of the American job conundrum. In fact, all of my worries had been eliminated. Breanna had accepted a job. I was about to begin a short-term project that would sustain me for a few months and anticipated being offered a job in the near future.

We were in the Caribbean town of Boca's Del Toro, literally the mouth of the bull, when we stumbled upon an Internet café down the street from a coconut stand. First, we bought some bomb ass coconuts for a quarter each and slurped the juice down while we climbed the stairs to the balcony Internet café. I logged into my email account, sorted through the junk, and skimmed over the rest. I received one email from the dude in San Antonio. It explained that his attorney had advised him against outsourcing business writing, in other words our deal was canceled. Fuck!

Fuck!

I actually said that out loud. I had funded my trip to Panama with money that I hadn't even earned yet.

His concern was that I could potentially do some work and take off with the research; using his ideas to begin my own business and market my own line of work gloves with room for long fingernails.

His concern wasn't entirely unrealistic, but I didn't understand why we couldn't just sign a contract stating that I would be acting in agency for the dude and that all work would be for him and his company. Instead, all the email said was that I was off the project.

After two fantastic weeks in Panama, we returned to Texas. Breanna and I moved into a house in San Antonio and she began her position.

ANOTHER BANK INTERVIEW

Somehow I came across a position at large financial institution that sounded like the bomb. The bank had a military lending department where, in association with the government, they provided lending and services to the government abroad. The position was a rotational one, and included opportunities of relocating abroad. They were seeking a smart, fresh graduate with a creative mind who could generate ideas for the department as it adopted a more private business style of operation. The position would rotate through the finance and operation departments and, like all rotational positions, the bank and the employee would determine where the employee was to begin a career.

This position was mine. I grew up in the military and had lived in Germany as a kid. I have lived in Mexico. I have also traveled throughout Western Europe, which displayed that I would be able to quickly adjust when placed abroad. I had just completed an MBA. How much more practical and creative could a candidate be?

However, before I could interview, an outsourced recruiting organization needed to assess my skill level with Microsoft Access and Excel. It seemed to me that sometimes certain assumptions could be made. For example, everyone with an MBA at the very least knows how to use basic software like Access and Excel. Although I had all the education, they still needed proof that I could link a database and use a spreadsheet. That's like asking someone that has completed a doctoral dissertation if he knows how to type using a word processor. We are talking about fundamental skills; like speaking English. Anyway, I aced the tests with a hundred percent accuracy on Excel and a ninety-two percent on Access.

Shortly after that preliminary waste of time, I interviewed with a personnel representative in the military lending department. She was young and had a pleasant personality, although seemed a bit rigid. She asked me the standard questions that I have answered a hundred times since. Questions like "tell me of a time where you had to confront a supervisor," and "tell me of a time you multitasked." In return, I asked a few form questions to her that I have since asked at every interview. I have grown equally bored of thinking of new questions.

I asked, "What is the biggest problem that I will encounter," "why is this position open" and "can you describe the culture here."

After the question and answer session, I left a stack of sample work from my portfolio with the interviewer. That job was mine. I found out there were a couple of positions open and they were interviewing fifteen or so folks. I had an excellent chance at it. I was a fresh graduate, had an advanced degree, and was willing to accept the entry-level salary of only thirty grand a year. Yes, thirty grand, not including parking, for an MBA if you can believe that shit. Desperate times.

They told me that a decision would be made by the end of that week regarding who was going to proceed to the second round. I called them on Friday, and of course they said they needed more time to decide because all of the applicants were so strong. This is what happens during an employer's economy. The applicant pool is so strong that everyone considered is an excellent fit for the position. We all had experience, advanced degrees, and were hungry for work.

Another week went by and I placed another call to ask if there had been any progress, and the interviewer informed me that she could not give me that information. Only the outsourced human resource department could do that. I contacted the people who conducted the software exams and found out that I was not selected.

Come on? That meant that there was someone more qualified for that shit than me. I was both pissed off and completely baffled. I had an advanced degree, language skills, experience abroad, and a willingness to suck it up for a mere thirty grand. That decision was incomprehensible and this time I was determined to get a recount. The next day, I called and asked for every manager in the military lending department that I possibly could. Each call that I placed was directed to voicemail because all of the managers were in a meeting.

I just wanted to speak with whoever was responsible for the actual hiring. I knew that much too often, businesses put hiring and selecting into the hands of the human resources department and much too often the department doesn't know what to look for. They don't know what questions to ask and how to find a good fit for a position. I wanted to circumvent human resources, because I was absolutely positive that if I could talk to a hiring manager, persuade them to listen to my concerns, that they would realize that I was indeed a qualified candidate.

About an hour later, I received two calls. One was from the outsourced human resources, and the other from the woman that had interviewed me. They were both agitated, not to mention confused, and had been contacted by the managers I had called that morning. "I don't know what you are trying to do Jon, but I am the one responsible for selecting the candidates," the interviewer told me.

Fuck.

Sometimes persistence actually gets you nowhere, but you must exhaust all possible alternatives. I apologized.

"I just feel you made an erroneous decision," I told them.

The interviewer said that she would recommend me for a "personal banker" position. Personal bankers are the ones sitting at desks in banks that open accounts and talk to you about various savings options and shit.

"Thanks," I said facetiously.

"Fuck that," I thought.

THIRTY GRAND
WORTH OF PASSION

After relocating to San Antonio with Breanna, I decided to target the local job market more heavily. On a daily basis I would check postings on the UT Austin job board and apply to everything I could, regardless of whether I was overqualified or interested in the position. I would apply to so many positions that I would forget many of the positions I had applied for, and I stopped taking the time to research companies beforehand.

One morning while on my laptop doing the same job searching shit that I had been doing for months, I received a call. "Hello Jon, I wanted to see if you were available to interview with us tomorrow for the position of investment associate," said a partner of an Austin-based investment firm.

"Certainly," I replied.

I did a little research online and refreshed my memory of the job posting. They were looking for someone smart, with a business background, to learn the company from top to bottom. The opening was a high profile position with daily direct contact with executives in the organization. The position had a career track of portfolio manager and the pay range was twenty-five to thirty thousand.

In my second semester of graduate school, I knew a couple of graduating MBA students who had accepted jobs with salaries in the mid-fifties. I never imagined that two years later, I would have to consider a position with a salary range of twenty-five to thirty grand. Times are tough.

The next morning I prepared my portfolio, which consisted of making copies of MBA coursework to leave for the interviewers, put on a nice suit, and was on my way. It is a long ass drive to Austin from San Antonio if you get stuck in traffic. The interview was on a Friday, and Fridays in Austin are notorious for hella traffic. The seventy-two mile drive took me about two hours. The office was located in the scenic hills of Austin and when I showed up, I was directed by the receptionist to wait in the boardroom. The boardroom had an incredible view of the Austin skyline, was well furnished, and had beautiful black and white photographs on the walls. If nothing else, these guys had taste.

Fifteen minutes later, a casually dressed man entered the room and introduced himself to me. He was the one that called me to set up the interview. We exchanged a little small talk and then begin discussing the position and how I would fit in. He gave me some background information about himself and his associates, and told me all about the company. The entire company only consisted of seventeen people. It was not departmentalized, meaning that there weren't marketing departments or finance departments; everybody did everything. He was one of the executives.

"It's not uncommon for me to get you coffee or to carry boxes," he told me. I was tempted to interrupt the interview and ask him to go get me a coffee at that point, but thankfully I kept that to myself.

"There is a steep learning curve here, Jon." He continued, "I want whoever is going to be offered this position to learn everything there is to know about this organization, in order to prepare them for a management role."

I explained my background and what my own interests were and where I wanted to be professionally. We connected on the fact that we both had spent some time in New York City: He grew up there and I spent many summers there with my family. I was playing any card I could to get offered that position. We hit it off. I came across as intelligent, calm, confident, and goal-oriented.

I went through a few of my form questions, such as "what is the evaluation process like," and "can you describe some of the difficulties that I may encounter?"

When we finished, the second interviewer came in. This guy was much younger, probably not over thirty. He told me of his background, about how he graduated from UT Austin and first moved to New York to work in the investment industry. This guy was particularly interested in how familiar I was with the bond market and he asked me to tell him what I knew. My answer would have made my undergraduate finance professor proud.

"Bonds have a face value, most pay a coupon rate, they are more attractive for safe investors who need a stream of annuities, they are long term investments, and so on."

He was unimpressed. "How familiar are you with bonds?" he asked.

"I understand how they are valued, and I understand the basics, but at this point I do not invest and my exposure has been through school."

I found it strange that this dude would grill me so hard for a position that paid as little as it did, especially when they weren't trying to hire an analyst. They were looking for an investment associate that they would train from the ground up. My time with the second interviewer didn't go terribly well, but fuck it. How much better are the other candidate's responses going to be?

When we finished, the third and final interviewer entered the boardroom. This guy was the coolest and most personable of all three. He basically just wanted to meet me and get an idea of what kind of person I was. He told me of the relaxed culture and the intense work that the company offers.

"The dress is casual, the people are all cool and smart, but as an investment associate you can't take a shit without the team knowing about it. We're also all friends, and it's not uncommon for us all to go out to Hooters and get wings."

This guy and I hit it off. I asked him about the other candidates and what they were like, and he filled me with confidence by recommending that if I wrote a strong thank you letter I shouldn't have any problems. The final decision was to be made in the following week.

Taking his advice, the next day I wrote thank you letters to all three of the guys who interviewed me.

The following week came and my phone didn't ring. Fuck. The anticipation was the worst part; I hate to wait. There are so many "what if" scenarios that start to play out in my head that being in a state of limbo makes me very anxiety-ridden. I called to follow up with the main guy who had more weight in the decision and was transferred to his voicemail.

"I just wanted to know where you guys are at in the decision process. I also wanted to reiterate my interest in the position," I said.

I called again a couple of hours later, this time to speak with the coolest of the three and actually got him on the phone. "No decision has been made; we will get back to you by Wednesday of next week," he told me.

Wednesday came and went and again I hadn't heard from them. I repeated my call to the main guy and left him another voicemail, then called the cool guy. Once again, he told me that a decision had not been made.

This was ridiculous. By this time I figured that I must not have been selected, or why else would the main dude be such a pussy? At the end of the week my suspicion was confirmed when I finally received an email from him. It was in that form letter format that I was becoming way too familiar with. "Although we found your skills and background to be impressive, we are moving forward with another candidate."

At this point I was months into the job search. I couldn't figure it out. I have an MBA, I am smart, I am multilingual, I dress well, I interview well, and I am hungry. I replied to the deciding guy via and asked him if he could give me feedback on my interview so that I may improve the next time.

He emailed back, stating that they liked me and were impressed, but felt that I wasn't passionate enough about the position. He then went on to state that they received seventy résumés and conducted twenty interviews. There were such passionate candidates that said shit like "all I want is a shot at this position," and "I will work for free for three months until I prove myself."

There is a fine line between confidence and desperation. One must relay that they can perform the functions of the position, as well as express their desire for the position. At the time of the interview, I felt that it would compromise my character if I were to suggest some outrageous shit like "I will work for free," and "all I want for Christmas is this opportunity."

Fuck them. If they couldn't see through the "I will say absolutely anything to get across that I want this job" bullshit, than they were probably a company that I didn't want to work for in the first place.

Three weeks later I checked the UT Austin job board as I always did and the same company appeared with a posting for the investment associate position once again. I guess that the person they selected, who would give them all hand jobs and work for pizza crusts, bounced when he got a more attractive offer. I inferred this because the pay window was no longer a mere twenty-five to thirty grand; they upped the ante to thirty to thirty-five.

FOOD SERVICE HELL

One of my first interviews after relocating to San Antonio was with a food delivery company that distributes foodstuffs all across Texas to schools and other cafeterias. The position was for a process analyst, and I found it on the UT Austin website.

This was by far the driest and most humorless company that I have ever interviewed with. I arranged an interview with the receptionist who, by the sound of her voice, complete despised her job. The company was located in an ugly industrial part of the San Antonio area, hella far north from where I was living downtown. I arrived, as always, wearing a nice suit and carrying my portfolio. To enter the building, visitors had to be buzzed into the front office. I pushed the buzzer and explained to the job-hating receptionist that I was there for the interview and she let me in. Inside, she threw me an evil glance as if I used to make fun of her in high school or something.

I was instructed to fill out an official application on a computer before I was to speak with anyone. After that, I was greeted by a young woman and asked to follow her to her office. She then explained the position and the company.

The company was originally formed and still operated by a family. The process analyst position would involve analyzing operations and make the business better, finding ways to improve efficiency and save costs, and other shit. We talked for a while and she asked me if I had time to speak with someone else, higher up in the hierarchy. She gave me a visitor pass and told me to ride a company van over to the distribution plant.

The distribution plant had the same process. I arrived and had to fill out a visitor form and wait in the waiting area. Again, I encountered unfriendly folks. If the folks working the frontline are disgruntled, what does that say about the company's culture? I waited for a few minutes browsing through the food distribution industry magazines that were on the table. There are magazines for everything.

A young guy of roughly my age came down and introduced himself. Now that I passed the first step, he was going to interview me. We walked up some stairs and through a few empty rooms that were furnished in the cheapest, blandest, most cost-effective manner I have ever seen. We ended up in a cold room and sat at a table. He then studied my résumé, as if it were the first thing he had ever read. Most interviewers that I had met with before then had utilized my résumé as a tool for the foot in the door. Management glances at the skill sets and education only as an introduction to begin the question and answer process. However, this asshole sat there scrutinizing my résumé for like ten minutes and all of his questions were simply to iron out the confusion he felt from reading that piece of paper representing my life's achievements.

"So you worked from this month to this month?" he asked. "What have you been doing since you graduated?"

"I have been looking for a job," idiot.

Judging from the frontline attitudes, the lack of people skills within management, and from the painfully boring surroundings, I knew that if I accepted any job at this place it would only be temporary.

This interviewer was the least skilled I had ever encountered. It was almost as if he didn't believe my education because he asked me to fax him all of my transcripts. He also told me that they were interviewing thirty-five candidates for the process analyst position.

What a waste of time. If I were already employed as the process analyst, I would have advised them to streamline the interview process, saving time and resources on whole procedure.

After the interview I left and this time I actually didn't even want the offer. I could never handle working in such a boring, humorless environment. However, I didn't want to eliminate it as an option, so the next day I faxed that dude my college transcripts. I never heard from him since. I guess that I am no longer being considered.

READ ANY GOOD
BOOKS LATELY?

When I was not selected for the operations position within the military lending department of the second bank, the outsourced human resources recruiter got the idea that I would be a good candidate for a sales position. Because I expressed an interest in the rotational overseas position in operations, then I would surely be interested in a position where I opened checking accounts for folks. It makes perfect sense.

I researched the personal banker role. Basically the role is a simple one: to deepen client relationships by informing current and potential customers on the products and services offered by the bank. A few weeks later I received a phone call from a representative with the bank in Austin. She said that according to my résumé I would possibly soar as a personal banker.

"Tell me a little about yourself," she asked.

I went on about how I was a first generation college student and had little direction as an undergraduate. I majored in anthropology because I found it very interesting and considered pursuing a doctorate in the area. My older brother, Brian, was pursuing his doctorate around the time I was deciding what to do after college. I saw first-hand his many trials and tribulations in his pursuit of the degree. Going the distance like that in a field like anthropology could be very narrowly focused, time consuming, and might have only prepared me for a career in teaching. Therefore, I wasn't convinced that was the direction I wanted to take. After college, I worked as a tour manager for an adventure tour company based in California. It was then that I identified my skills in leading teams, as it was my responsibility to lead groups of international tourists throughout North America. I demonstrated great leadership qualities and enjoyed working in the groups.

Ever since college, I always knew that I was bound for an advanced degree, but was undecided as to what to pursue. I had an interest in learning about finance and international markets, so I eventually decided to get an MBA. It took me three years, instead of the regular two, due to the fact that I had to take undergraduate courses in business before I could advance to graduate work. In school, and from projects that I would do on the side, I discovered that I had a passion for problem solving. I thrived in areas such as statistics, finance, and operations. I always took a lead in my teams.

Actually, I probably told her a more condensed version of that, but you get it all.

"Do you have any experience in sales?" she asked.

"I have never worked in sales directly, but I have extensive customer service and client relationship experience," I answered.

"Do you want to go into sales?"

Now, this is where I fucked up. I told her that I had never really thought about it, but would consider it depending on the company and position. She asked if I felt that I could develop a passion in this area. I told her that my philosophy of life is that one must experience something first and, based on that experience, either change directions or continue. How am I to know what I will love to do in the future if I have such limited exposure to the different areas? Whether I develop a diet of grapefruit for the rest of my life really depends on how I feel about the first bite.

She didn't like that at all.

"We are seeking those who are passionate about sales, and those who want to develop a life long career in sales," she said.

I repeated my philosophy, as if she hadn't understood me earlier. I believe that one has to be exposed to something before a passion can be generated. I told her that I liked the aspects of sales that I was familiar with, such as meeting people and providing solutions, via products and services, to people.

We actually started to argue a bit from this point.

"Jon," she addressed me as if we were buddies, "Tell me your ideal position."

I told her I could only speak in abstracts because my scope had not yet been narrowed down. I went on about how my ideal position would be intellectually stimulating, have upward mobility, be dynamic enough to adapt to the environment, would allow me to utilize my existing skills and develop new ones, would involve analysis, and a few other things.

Her reply was stifling, and gave me some clue as to her nature, and the nature of the position she was calling about. "Jon, visit monster.com and tell me how many job descriptions match what you just told me."

We were no longer discussing the personal banker position that I would soar with. She suggested that I narrow the scope of my interests to a position and progress from there, recommending that I read a book by Richard Bolles called *What Color is Your Parachute*. She said that it would be a useful tool for me to narrow my interests. She also suggested that I do temporary work in a variety of areas to gain some exposure. All this great advice from someone that initially called to interview me for a position I had no interest in.

Because we were now exchanging book recommendations, I told her to check out *The Unbearable Lightness of Being*, by Milan Kundera, where life is defined as a sketch comedy. It is a sketch because we make it up as we go along. Nobody has ever gone in the exact path as any particular individual, therefore we can never truly know what to expect. Life is constantly being made by our decisions and choices. I can imagine wanting to be a physician, but I will never know what it would be like without actually being a one first. Even with watching shows like *ER*, and hearing testimonials, one can never know.

Life is also a comedy. All of our basic necessities have generally been met and all of this other shit is strictly for comedic value. The fact that we are so insignificant in the grand scheme of things makes our lives and decisions not matter at all. I think it's funny that people will spend fifty grand on a Hummer, and then have to work for years at a marketing department to pay it off. Over the course of our history, we have created a world that just doesn't make sense. Generally speaking, we all have enough to eat and we all have shelter. All of the other shit in our lives is superfluous.

Again, I probably said less than that. I also realized that the discussion was going south early on when she indicated she was looking for someone with a passion for sales. I wasted the better part of an hour on my cell phone with that whack job. Shit, I only got six hundred minutes a month.

WATCH OUT

Although physically close to Austin, San Antonio is culturally another world. Well, maybe not another world, but at least another decade. San Antonio is an economically depressed, sprawling blue-collar city. The area is home to a million and a half people and it has one of the largest Hispanic populations in the country. It is obvious to anyone that visits anywhere in the city, other than the tourist-oriented river walk and Alamo, that the town lacks economic vitality. There is no concentrated cluster of nightlife, as is usually encountered in developed cities. In fact, all of the nightlife spots are found in strip malls. There are a couple of cool coffee shops and a monthly art festival, but overall the town kind of sucks.

At San Antonio's public university, the University of Texas at San Antonio, I spoke with a representative from a "financial planning" company. I asked him what sorts of opportunities were available and pretended to be interested when he told me the usual "we are looking for salespeople" pitch. By this point, I was in no position to be choosy, so I lied and said that it interested me. I heard from him a few days later and he wanted me to come in to talk so that I could get a better idea of the position and the company. He suggested an early ass interview time of eight in the morning for some crazy reason and, for some crazier reason, I agreed.

I arrived and met the dude for an interview in another boardroom. He gave me some background on the company, it's the biggest this-and-that company with a great strategy of doing this-and-that, and they are better than their competitors due to blah, blah, and blah.

"It's great that you are interested," he told me.

"You are very educated and it is obvious that you are qualified." He went on to explain that their brand of financial planners don't need a graduate degree, hell, they don't even need a college degree. He also explained that there was absolutely no base salary for this position. Compensation was one hundred percent commission. It was one of these "you can make nothing or up to six figures" deals. In addition, there was absolutely no clientele set in place. The unpaid financial planners had to get their own clientele.

"It's all networking," he said. "You plan the finances of your friends, their friends, their parents, and their coworkers."

I thought about all of my friends and how they would totally look at me like "what the fuck?" if I were to talk about streams of annuities with them. There is something about selling insurance that just seems boring and the pure commission-based system turned me off. It reminded me of pyramid schemes and shit. This wasn't a job it was a scam. Given that, it was no surprise that this dude loved me. It was quite obvious that he was a salesman the way he was determined to get an answer out of me. This was the job that I wanted the least.

"So whaddaya think?" he asked me, as he was excited to have me on board.

He also provided the analogy of interviewing being like dating. "First there is the preliminary information exchange stage, which is what we have here and then there is the decision as to if there should be a second date, which I definitely want," he said.

Was this dude coming on to me? Was he asking me on a second date? Anyway, I told him that it was nice to meet him and left. That was on a Friday.

On Monday I received calls from that dude and he left one message. He explained how he was anxious to move the process along. I never called him back. The next day he called eight times and I never answered. The motherfucker didn't even limit his calls to the daytime hours. When the phone rang at nine in the evening, I answered it to bring this chapter to an end, or who knows how long the calls may have continued. I once met a crazy girl from Portland who called me every fifteen minutes, for four hours, and left a message each time. I told him that I really couldn't take a "job" that was so janky. He never called back.

BREANNA

We moved to San Antonio because Breanna accepted an offer as a pricing coordinator with a huge financial company. Now that she was employed, she had access to internal job postings with her company. They would frequently come through her work email, and she would let me know when there were any opportunities that I would be interested in. She would forward postings to my personal email account and I would send in my résumé. One day, I actually received a call.

I had applied internally for an analyst position. A new position was to be created under the finance umbrella for someone that could analyze shit was interested in starting a career with the company. It was an entry-level position, which was the only way an outsider could get a foot in the door with that fucking company. Their philosophy, much like what I was experiencing everywhere else, was to hire from within. That meant that everyone had to start at an entry-level position.

I was very excited when I received the phone call. Since moving to San Antonio, I had been contacted by a total of zero companies I was actually interested in working for. I'll admit that by this point I would have accepted anything, but when the economy recovered I would bounce as soon as possible. This company was different. Breanna seemed to really enjoy her job and she was getting paid well. Her company was active in the community and was a heavy contributor to charitable organizations such as United Way. I actually became happy now that I had a glimmer of hope for a decent job. I started thinking of how Breanna and I could carpool to work and everything, how cute.

Before the interview, I prepared like a sonofabitch. They were going to offer me the job; they simply had no choice in the matter. I was going to go in there and perform with such passion, such integrity, and such intellect that they were going to have no choice but to hire me.

The interview came and again I brought my leather portfolio with me to leave some projects with the interviewer. I had a nice, dark grey suit on and I had just gotten a fresh hair cut. I was absolutely determined to nail this one. I knew that company from front to back. I studied all of Breanna's literature about their history and philosophy. I knew the position and I wanted it, bad. I arrived to their building and the receptionist told me to have a seat as someone would be right down to speak with me. A few minutes later, a young man who looked about my age, but bald, introduced himself to me. We shook hands walked to his office. During the small talk, he asked me how I had heard of the position. I was afraid he'd ask that and had a response prepared just in case.

"Probably online, that's where I usually find jobs," I told him. I didn't want to reveal that an insider had forwarded me the notification.

I took a seat in his office and experienced a repeat of every other interview that I had up to that point, same format and questions. By then, I had enough practice to be an expert interviewee. I knew what my responses would be before the questions were even asked. I was professional, friendly, confident, and passionate. He was impressed by my responses, portfolio, knowledge of the company, and passion. The interview went perfectly. I tactfully and intelligently answered every question and I asked appropriate counter questions. At the conclusion, I let him know that I had been following the company for years and had targeted it as the primary company in San Antonio that I was interested in.

The next morning I sent him a letter, thanking him for his time and reiterating my desire to work for the company. After a week, I received a letter from them in the mail and quickly opened it, looking forward to the good news.

"You were a very strong candidate, but unfortunately we chose to pursue another candidate."

Not again.

I was devastated and equally pissed off. I couldn't believe how this could have happened. I knew that company like an employee. My interview was fantastic. There was no doubt in my mind that they weren't going to extend me the offer. Hell, it was an entry-level piece position after all. There must have been some mistake. I immediately attempted to call the interviewer, whose signature was at the bottom of the rejection letter, but received his voicemail. I left a message about how I was confused and couldn't understand why I was not chosen. I wanted them to reconsider. I sent an email that same day explaining that I sincerely wanted to work for them and that I would appreciate if he could forward my résumé on to other departments.

When Breanna returned home, I was distraught. I had been looking for a job for months and my self-esteem and confidence were now at an all time low. I needed a job. I needed money. I needed to be a man. I need to be a man with money. A man's sense of value and worth is directly related to his occupation, and I was feeling worthless. The light at the end of the tunnel was at a weak flicker. I was overwhelmed with confusion. Breanna couldn't understand why I was passed over except that maybe they went with a current employee.

She helped get me more contacts within the company so that I could explore every possible avenue. I had over twenty names of department heads and emailed each of them. I informed them of how I interviewed for a position and had not been selected but I wanted to work for them so passionately that I would be willing to come in as an intern. I asked them to please notify me of any available opportunities and to forward my résumé to different departments. I attached a cover letter including a summary of my background so they would feel comfortable forwarding my résumé. I received a few responses that said that they had indeed forwarded my résumé. A few days later, I received an email from the person that had originally interviewed me. According to his email, he was confused.

"I am not sure why you are contacting so many departments, but please stop it. I am not sure what is going on, but I have received a total of four of your résumés forwarded to me. I will let you know if something becomes available."

I emailed that dude back and explained how it was not my intention to flood his inbox with résumés and that I was simply exploring other departments. It was my belief that persistence usually pays off.

ANOTHER WASTE OF TIME

While drinking a beer with a friend at the Triple Crown pub in San Marcos, I received a phone call on my cell. "This is Jon," I answered.

"Hello Jon, my name is James Ramirez. I am calling about your résumé," he explained.

He reminded me of a marketing manager position that I had apparently applied for through the UT Austin job board. I was applying for dozens of jobs every day then, so it was difficult for me to remember if I had applied to this one. He said that he was particularly interested in my statistical simulations experience and wanted to get together in the following week. He was planning on being in San Antonio that Monday and we made arrangements to meet at a well-known Mexican restaurant for lunch. After talking with the guy, I checked my email and remembered the applying for the position. Then, I looked at their confusing website. It was extremely vague as to what exactly the company did, but it appeared to look like they sold health products.

That Monday, when I arrived at the restaurant, I wasn't sure what to expect from this meeting other than a free lunch. I thought it was interesting that the reason he chose to meet me was because of my simulation projects. Maybe he was interested in a forecasting project or something like that. My uncertainty was fueled by the fact that the job posting was vague and the website was confusing.

I arrived on time and waited at the bar. Mr. Ramirez arrived fifteen minutes late. We shook hands and sat down at a table where we both ordered some greasy Mexican food and engaged in some small talk. He noticed on my résumé that I had lived in Mexico, so that led to a brief conversation about my favorite town in the world, Guanajuato.

After the small talk got old, we began a conversation about his company and the position. This motherfucker goes on in the vaguest terms ever and about five minutes in to his monologue, I figured out that I no longer wanted to hear any more. He went on about how in his company "you create your own communities of clientele," and "build your own base." This asshole had the audacity to invite me to that restaurant and try to recruit me for yet another pyramid scheme. I became furious.

"Dude, the position you are describing and the 'marketing manager' position that you posted sound like two completely different things," I said.

"No, you have got it all wrong. You have to market yourself to attract people that want to work for you. You can organize your own organizations."

What the fuck was this dude talking about? Organize your own organizations? I asked him about how he specifically made reference to my statistical simulation experience, and he replied that he sought out intelligent people to join his team. Statistics, apparently, indicated that I was bright.

Yes, I was bright, too bright to be roped into his scam.

My job hunt had been steadily worsening. I was pissed that I had just finished an MBA and found myself sitting at a crappy greasy food joint listening to the ridiculous shit exiting this fool's mouth. I threw my napkin on the table and got up. "Mr. Ramirez, this has been a complete waste of my time," I said as I walked out.

What was it about my résumé that indicated I would be a good candidate for a pyramid scheme? This was my second interview that turned out to be an attempt to get me into such a business. The goal of pyramid businesses is to employ as many people as possible regardless of their experiences. To someone within a pyramid, everyone is seen as suckers. They typically sucker people into what can be a "make your own hours," "be your own boss," or "make up to six figures in your first year" business opportunity. They prey upon anyone whose rational thinking will be blinded by the possibility of riches and empowerment. The reality, however, is pretty sad. Pyramids thrive on making everyone in the pyramid distribute and market the company's products. They offer folks no money and no clientele. All they do is convince you that you can sell their products to your friends and employ them to be distributors of the same products. When you have suckered someone in with the false dreams of making millions independently, you have then advanced a layer in the scheme.

This dude suckered me into a meeting because he claimed to like my simulation experience but only wanted me to sell products for him in the same manner, just like the janky "financial planner" scheme that didn't require a college degree. I am disgusted by the sales tactic of ambiguity. All pyramids use the same tactic, and they all attempt to convince their prey that they are recruiting for a marketing and sales entrepreneurial opportunity. What it basically comes down to is having other people sell your products while you earn a percentage.

WE LOVE SERVERS!

I knew of an MBA candidate that dropped out of the program early on because he didn't want to pursue the degree any longer and he accepted a job with a rental car company. I figured that any full-time position worthy of abandoning graduate school for had to be a good one. Although I did consider that maybe he had dropped out because he really wasn't that bright or was complacent and played the default game. Maybe he just realized that the time and money investment in a third-tier bidness skool just wasn't worth it.

I thought about this one day while I was at the computer, like always. I visited company's website to learn about them and the opportunities that they might have available. I discovered that they only hired for basically one entry-level position, and then promote from within. The position was called "manager in training" and the website described it as a fast-paced, cross-departmental position for which they sought out candidates with a variety of backgrounds. Those who succeeded in the management training program would eventually run their own rental office. They would select their own employees and have a certain freedom with marketing and so on.

The entrepreneurial aspect of the position interested me. I had completed business plans and thrived on developing and strategically positioning businesses. They didn't accept uploaded résumés, so I spent the greater portion of an hour filling in my educational background, professional experience, and answering their other form questions. I got an emailed response that same day.

"That's pretty timely," I thought.

I opened the email and it stated that I lacked customer service experience and therefore would not be considered. My MBA meant nothing. My experience as a statistician and researcher meant nothing. My two years of group leading in the Third World meant nothing. My Spanish language skills meant nothing. This made me confused. Why would customer service experience matter more than my other, more specialized, qualifications?

Desperate for anything, I replied immediately and informed them that many of my jobs prior to graduate school, such as working as a tour guide, were in customer service. I also mentioned that while I spent a summer living in New York I worked as a server at a restaurant. I mentioned that I had cashiering experience. I also pointed out that sometimes certain assumptions can be made, like inferences from my project experience, education, and teaching skills would make me a likely candidate to work well with customers. Finally, I included in the body of the email the question, "should I include my experience as a waiter on this application?"

What I hate about human resource departments is that sometimes they make terrible decisions based on rigid criteria. I would suggest to any company, when trying to fill professional level positions, eliminate the human resource departments and actually have assistants for the deciding management act in the selection process.

Five minutes later she replied. "Yes definitely include any experience as a server, we love servers!"

This all should have been a serious red flag, but I was extremely frustrated with my job search and getting more and more desperate. I resubmitted the online application, this time including the summer job where I brought plates of food from the kitchen to my tables and filled glasses of water.

Hard to believe, but that got me an interview.

The interview was scheduled for the following Monday. I learned everything I could about renting cars, I prepared complete portfolio, and I wore a nice suit. I arrived to the San Antonio headquarters where I was greeted by the receptionist, who happened to be the person that I had been corresponding with. "He will be right down to see you," she informed me as she asked me to pin a visitor tag on my lapel.

A few minutes later a tall, amicable man in a black suit neared me with his arm extended. "Hello, I am Bill. You must be Jon," he said as he shook my hand.

We walked back to his office, engaging in light chit-chat about the day.

During the interview he asked me why I wanted the position. I responded like I had wanted to work for them ever since I was a small child. While other children wanted to be astronauts and firemen; I wanted to be a rental car manager.

"I admire the business model," I actually answered.

I went on to state that I had been following this company for years and I was attracted to its intentions, innovations and ability to remain one of the benchmarks in the industry. I respected how everyone begins at the entry-level and how that gives them all the knowledge base and the cross functionality necessary to truly know and believe in the company. The company was well positioned and I admired the fact that once managers in training make the transition into management they are empowered to make decisions based on what they deem appropriate. It was my goal to move into a management or entrepreneurial role and that was exactly what they were about. Furthermore, I had a good friend (actually, I never spoke to the guy in my life) who quit graduate school because this was such a fantastic company to work for.

Bill was honestly impressed by my tone and knowledge. I could tell by his reaction.

"Because we are a customer service company, our hours revolve around the customer," he said. "Therefore work hours will be until six or later, depending on the location, and on Saturdays."

"That's fine," I responded immediately.

"The average manager in training will usually be expected to work close to 50 hours a week and will begin with a salary of around twenty-seven thousand," he continued.

"Fine," I immediately responded.

During this interview, I reminded myself of the character George Costanza, from the show *Seinfeld*. My intense desire to work for this company was similar to episode in which George was interviewed for a salesman position with a brassiere company. He went on about how since he was a kid he had loved bras and had always wanted to work in the field. A Costanza-style deception was exactly what I was doing for this rental company. It was basic survival mode. One must have an income to live, and in an employer's market passion can make the difference.

During the "would you like to ask us anything" portion of the interview, I asked about other possible career tracks.

"I was a manager for thirteen years, and now I am the regional hiring director for the area. You can also go into operations, finance, marketing, and just about any department," he continued.

When I asked about how many candidates I was up against, he furnished me with a very interesting reply. He claimed that they hire when they feel somebody is a good fit, not just when there is a specific position to fill. "The company is growing and we need as many managers as possible to grow, so if there are forty qualified applicants then I hire all forty."

I handed him copies of certain items in my portfolio. "Here is a copy of the business plan that I completed," I said. I thought it might impress him to know that I have managed a team and had a thorough understanding of positioning, benchmarking, research, and analysis.

I also gave him a report I had done in an advanced statistics class. I was given a ton of data on a hundred different models of cars and, using advanced statistical techniques, I created a model that showed which factors were most responsible for determining how many miles per gallon a car would get. Although heavy on the technical side, he seemed impressed with the report.

I also gave him copies of my recommendation letters. He was genuinely impressed and, as I left, I felt assured that I would get this offer. I sent a thank you letter the next day, again reiterating my desire to become a part of the team.

Two days later I received a letter from him in the mail. I was so confident that I would be offered the position, that I opened the letter with anticipation of finally having a job.

"Unfortunately, we have decided to move on with other candidates…" the letter said and thanked me for my time.

I couldn't believe it.

I sat in this guy's office just two days earlier as he told me that their system didn't work like that. They hired on fit basis, not by the number of available positions, and yet the letter was personally signed by him. I was amazed that he didn't remember discussing that very concept with me.

Confused, angry, and yet a little relieved, I sent him an email. I was confused and angry for obvious reasons. However, I was relieved because although I was desperate, I really didn't want to sell myself short for the twenty-seven grand, fifty-hour workweek, working on Saturdays job at what was basically a retail sales counter. There was no reply.

Months later, I attended a career fair at the University of Texas in San Antonio. The fair was very similar to the one at Southwest Texas; filled with less prestigious companies seeking to fill less interesting positions than the one at UT Austin. I noticed that Bill was there, recruiting for the same management training program. He had the same goofy smile and was talking to students in the same excited manner, as he did when I first spoke with him. Still pissed off that he never responded to my inquiries, I approached him. I reminded him of whom I was and then asked him again about why they decided to not move forward with me. I also asked why he seemingly contradicted himself by one day telling me that their hiring policy was based on fit, not the number of open positions, and then moving forth with another candidate.

"We felt that you just weren't a good fit with the organization."

MORE FUN WITH CARS

One day my girlfriend was talking with an old friend that she worked with while still in school. The topic of my situation inevitably surfaced, and the friend mentioned that her husband had recently made a very successful career change. He left the world of engineering for a job as a car buyer for a new dealership. Trying to explore every possibility, Breanna asked her friend to put him and I in contact with each other.

A few days later, her husband called me and explained what he did and that he absolutely loved it. His was a "buyer in training," which meant that he purchased cars for his Houston office from other dealerships, private sellers, and from auctions around the country. From his enthusiasm and from my total desperation for work, I asked him if he would forward my résumé to whoever was in charge of the San Antonio office.

About a week later I received a call from a recruiter, also based out of the Houston office, who was in charge of the initial screening and recommending phases. He asked me for some preliminary information and told me that I came highly recommended (which was great, considering it was by the husband of a friend of my girlfriend). He told me about the company, which was a relatively new chain of used car dealerships. They bought cars, sold cars, and even serviced cars. The thing that made them stand out from other used car dealerships was that the cars had to go through rigorous testing.

All the cars on their lots were good, solid cars under warranty. They were proud of the fair relationships they have with their customers. They didn't bargain, they offered a set price when buying a car and asked a set price when selling, and their salespeople were informative rather than aggressive.

I said that it sounded like a great company and an excellent opportunity that I would likely love. That was actually true. I told him about my background and then he requested that I email him my résumé.

"Well, I actually have a website specifically designed for employers," I told him. "You can download my résumé, and you can download some of my projects if you like, so that you can get an idea of my logic, experience, and writing skills."

For some reason he refused to look at my website, claiming that he wanted to avoid any bias when assessing potential candidates.

What the fuck was he talking about? As I told this dude, the purpose of my website was to provide potential employers information and examples from my portfolio of MBA coursework. I learned special software skills to design it and paid almost ten bucks a month to make it available. In the past, it had been an impressive tool for me to get information to employers and helped me stand out from the crowd. What bias was this guy talking about? Bias refers to some sort of unfair preference in decision-making. If looking at my website would bias his assessment of me as a candidate, then so would my education, my experience, or any of the other accomplishments listed on my résumé. Did he also not want to know if I had an MBA or had completed research projects in order to avoid this bias? Successfully applying for a job means creating a preference for your skills over those of the other candidates. Employers have to be biased in choosing the best possible applicants. That is simply the way it works. Besides, it wasn't like my website had links to porn or political organizations; it was just my résumé and a few projects. I was amazed that this dude refused to learn more about me.

About a week later we set up a first round phone interview. "It should take about an hour," he said, and as always I prepared as much as possible. I probably learned more about the company than some of their employees.

On the phone, it felt as if I had already had this interview before. It was like all corporations had access to the same question bank. "Tell me of a time where you made a suggestion for improvement to your superior." "Tell me of a time when you persuaded someone to change how they felt about something." "Tell me of a time that you took on a leadership role." It seemed that the questions were never going to end but finally, after an hour, it was my turn. I asked what possible career track the buyer in training position could lead to. I also asked about any transferable skills that I would learn.

His response was interesting. The career track for a buyer in training was to first become a buyer, which could take up to a year. After that, one could advance to buyer II and then to regional buyer. The career track seemed limited to achieving more and more prestige under the buyer umbrella. "You will also have exposure to financial reports, pricing, and accounting data," he said, "however your main responsibilities will be to buy inventory."

I told him I was interested and he informed me that he would review all of the candidates and then make recommendations.

Weeks went by and I didn't hear anything. I figured that they must have realized that I was not a good fit, because my areas of interests were in statistics and shit. Then, one day I was riding my bike through downtown San Antonio and I got a call asking me if I was still interested. Unemployed and desperate, I told said that I was glad to hear from them and would love to have the opportunity. We set up a time for me to go into the local San Antonio office. There, I would have to fill in an application and take several computer-assisted tests before I could be formally interviewed.

I showed up at the San Antonio office a few days later. I was wearing my black suit and had my portfolio. The receptionist handed me a big ass packet of forms to complete and, as usual, I had to manually write in my educational information, my residential information, and my references. That took about thirty minutes. All of that shit was already on my résumé, why couldn't they just accept résumés and quit wasting our time? I also had to sign an arbitration agreement, which I did. I returned the completed application back to the receptionist with a smile. She then walked me over to a computer room and set up the tests that I was to complete.

The first "test" asked for more detailed background information. I remember being completely amazed that I had already given them a résumé and turned in an application with the exact same information. It asked for specific dates from past employment and reminded me several times that all employees go through credit checks, criminal background checks, and verification checks for all past employers. It then asked if there were any additional positions that I had held in the past that were not reflected on the written application. Then, it requested the name of every company I had ever worked for, every position I had ever held, and my reason for leaving each of them.

What a complete waste of time.

I listed that I had worked as a social worker in Ohio for four months when I was temporarily living with my brother. I mentioned that I was a cashier for six months at a music store in Austin while finishing college. I was also a parking garage cashier for the University of Texas. I also worked in a pizza shop for a couple of years. None of these experiences were pertinent to the position I was applying to. Furthermore, this was the only company I encountered that required such information.

Although a waste, that section was not the worst by any means, the next one was. The next test took an hour to complete and consisted of personality questions obviously focused on revealing my moral or ethical structure. I was bothered that I had to answer these questions in the first place, but the style of the questions was horrible. Having expertise in survey design and techniques of analysis, I noticed that these questions were loaded and geared to get every bit of record for any dishonest behavior. Also, the test asked the same questions over and over again, obviously to check for consistency.

"We know that most people have experimented with marijuana in their lives. When was the last time that you used marijuana?"

"In a recent study it was discovered that ninety percent of the U.S. population has stolen something in their lives. When was the last time that you have ever taken something that wasn't yours?"

By their word choice, each of those questions assumes that the applicant has committed a crime. It was only in the response choices that one could indicate that they hadn't stolen or used drugs. I was offended by each question for the entire duration of the test. Besides, how many applicants would actually admit to a potential employer that they stole the latest Eminem CD last week? I responded to everything in a way that they would have liked a potential employee to answer. I had never done drugs, I had never taken anything that was not mine, I never associated with such people, and I would immediately report all thefts or suspicions of theft to my supervisor under any circumstances. The questions were structured to induce a forced confession.

The company could save time and resources if they would just conduct the drug and background tests that they repeatedly threatened in the first section.

After my computer time, I was greeted by a dude, whose job it was to collect more information before I could actually be interviewed. "What is this, the CIA," I thought. He took me into another room where he had the printouts of my computerized tests results. He informed me that he was the liaison between the applicant and the department head with whom I would be interviewing. He then asked me about any gaps in my employment record and specifically about all the positions I had just listed on the computer but felt compelled to leave off the written application.

"Rural Opportunities, tell me about that."

I went on about how I held a social worker position while living with my brother for a few months in Ohio. I explained how I led a program for Spanish speaking migrant farm workers and helped families with their communication. I added how the program's philosophy was that if youths could talk openly with their parents, they wouldn't turn to delinquent behavior.

"Why did you leave it?"

I told him I received another offer.

"Music Mania, tell me about that."

"I was a cashier at a record store called Music Mania," I said, repeating verbatim what I entered on the computer.

"Why did you leave it?"

I was a cashier. Who is a career cashier? I told him that I graduated from college and accepted a full-time offer in California.

"University of Texas, tell me about that."

"I was a cashier at UT," again I repeated the response readily available in his computer printout.

"Why did you leave it?"

By this point I thought that this motherfucker only knew two English phrases: "tell me about it" and "why did you leave it." I told him that I was a cashier and I accepted the job with the music store because the pay was better. We went through that whole process again for the last job on my list: Double Dave's Pizza.

He studied the gaps in my employment and asked about them. "I have been a full-time student until now you moron," I thought. I explained how as a student, I had not always been successful at finding flexible employment opportunities. We finally finished and he asked me to again wait in the lobby.

A few minutes later, a couple of dudes approached me with smiles on their faces and their arms extended to shake my hand.

"Hello Jon, I am the buying manager," he introduced himself.

Finally, after jumping through all those ridiculous hoops, I actually got to talk to this dude. He and a senior buyer invited me into yet another room and then interviewed me for an hour. They asked the usual shit and told me the usual shit. When it was my turn, I asked them the usual shit and told them the usual shit. I told them that I desired a position that was stimulating and interesting and had opportunities for advancement. I also told them I was impressed with everything I knew about the company and from what I had heard from my friend. I showed them a few letters of recommendation. They were impressed with my performance thus far. I explained how I wished to begin a career with them and that it was definitely the position I wanted.

They thanked me for going through all the hoops and asked me what I had thought of the computerized portion of the procedure. I tactfully told them that, although I understand the company needed to know that its employees were not drugged out thieves, the number of questions should be reduced and the style should be changed. Rather than simple questions, they were written as assumptions that the applicant has already committed these misdeeds. "I was personally offended by that format," I went on to say.

They appreciated my demeanor, professionalism, desire and abilities so much that they then took me on a tour of the facilities. They introduced me to everyone in the department and showed me the entire operation, which was actually quite interesting. They then insisted that I watch a buyer perform one of their functions; assessing the value of a used car and making an offer.

After a total of four hours, they asked if I was in a hurry because they wanted me to take yet another test and interview with other buyers. The test that they wanted to administer was to take about another two hours, but it turned out that they didn't have time to administer it. Therefore, we arranged for me to return the next day. Before I left, I asked how much of the interview process remained and how many candidates they were considering.

Similarly to rental agency, the manager told me that they did not hire a limited number of people. They were growing so fast, he told me, that he would hire forty people right now if all forty fit the bill.

I went back the next day and was administered the other test. This time it was a pencil-and-paper personality assessment. I spent over an hour answering questions about whether I was an extrovert or an introvert. After I finished, I asked to speak with a couple of the other buyers. I was told to wait in the lobby and that they would be right out. I ended up sitting there drinking their complimentary shitty coffee for a fucking hour and they never came out to talk to me. I tactfully told the receptionist that I would wait another fifteen minutes, but after that I would have to reschedule. Either meet with me or reschedule. These dudes knew that I was just sitting there in the lobby. Ten minutes later a buyer came over to me.

"Jack, right," he said.

"Jon, close though," I joked.

"Do you have an appointment or something to go to," he asked me.

I told him I had nothing pressing, but pointed out the fact that I had been waiting in the lobby for over an hour. "Oh," he said and hurriedly walked back in the direction from which he came. Fifteen minutes later he returned, accompanied by another buyer.

They made no apology for wasting my time and asked me to follow them for the interview. It was exactly the same interview as the day before except with two different guys. What a complete waste of time and energy I thought. They asked me the same shit and I told them the same shit that I said both in the phone interview and the day before. Again, the interview lasted an hour. One of the guys asked me if I could see myself working for them when I am forty years old. I said yes, as long as I felt that I was moving toward a goal.

In total, I spent about ten hours with that company. I thought for sure they were going to offer me the position; why else would they invest so much time and energy in talking to me and processing my tests? They all seemed genuinely impressed with me and we all hit it off.

Two weeks went by and I called the buying manager and got his voicemail. I left a message that I was still interested and that I was eager to progress in the process, and blah, blah, blah. I was called back that afternoon by the recruiter in Houston that I had the initial phone interview with. He informed me that although they were indeed impressed by my qualifications, they interviewed other candidates and felt I was not the best fit. Once again, contradicting the hiring philosophy that the buying manager had discussed with me a couple of weeks earlier. What a pussy way out of it.

IN THE DAY

Long before I even considered going to graduate school for my MBA, I finished college in anthropology and accepted the greatest job I would ever have: working as a tour guide for Suntrek Tours. During college, I had worked at a summer camp and I had learned about the company from some international counselors (networking!). A few English girls were planning on touring the east coast with them after finishing their summer at the camp. In my senior year of college, I knew I wasn't quite ready for graduate school nor was I ready to fall into a traditional job. Therefore, the tour guide job was ideal.

I flew out to San Francisco and caught a bus an hour north of the bay to a beautiful small town called Santa Rosa, where Suntrek Tours was headquartered. The company, along with a couple of competitors, had an interesting business. They provided adventure tours throughout the United States, Canada, Mexico, and Belize. The tourists were all international; mostly from Western Europe, Australia, and Asia. Suntrek's targeted market was young, single, and adventurous. Although Suntrek had no age restrictions for their tours, most tourists were between twenty to thirty-five years old.

Suntrek organized tours that ranged from one to six weeks with both camping and hotel stays. The tours provided an excellent mix of nature and cities and were a perfect way to get a balanced understanding of the country. All of the tours were conducted in fifteen passenger vans with up to thirteen passengers. The vans were fitted with custom-made roof racks so that the luggage and camping equipment could ride on top of the van while they were inside. It was tour guide's responsibility to drive the van, load and unload all luggage and equipment, set up the major components of camp, organize all lodging and activities, offer cultural and background information, and keep expense records. The guides were the only representative from the company that the tourists would have. The guides would pick up the tourists in one city, drive them around the country, and then drop them off in another city, sometimes even in another country.

My training lasted two weeks and included driving tests, simulated tour guiding, and van maintenance. I did very well, as did everyone else except for two who just didn't make the cut. One was neurotic and a horrible communicator in English. The other was an older American man who was attacked by a bear in Alaska several years earlier. He hated bears and regularly asked the general manager if he was ever in on a tour in Alaska could he encourage his tourists to carry guns. He also had a crazy documentation of his past experiences that he referred to as his résumé, consisting of nothing more than the dates he had traveled and when he was attacked.

My first tour was a one-week trip called the "Western Sun" that went from Los Angeles to San Francisco, hitting all of the hot spots in between including the Grand Canyon, Las Vegas, Yosemite National Park, Joshua Tree National Park, and other cool places. This tour was to be the first time I was ever to lead a group of people to places I that had never been to before. Luckily, this was a popular tour and there were other vans driving the same route. On the first day, I introduced myself to another guide, Mike, who told me to just follow him around so that I wouldn't get lost or off schedule.

I arrived at the hotel in Los Angeles and found a bunch of people sitting next to their backpacks in the lobby. Right away I knew they were my tourists. They were a diverse group of people: two young Belgian guys who were on their last leg of their tour around the world, a twenty-something Australian woman, a Korean family of four, a Vietnamese girl, and a few others. I introduced myself and behaved as confidently and enthusiastically as I could, masking the nervousness I felt.

The first thing on the agenda was to show this group around the city for a few hours before continuing on to Joshua Tree National Park to spend the night. The usual quick Los Angeles tour includes Hollywood Boulevard, a stop to view the Hollywood sign, a drive through Beverly Hills and Rodeo Drive, and a visit to Venice Beach.

Los Angeles was a mess. I got lost almost immediately after leaving the hotel and ended up driving around trying to find Hollywood way longer than it should have taken. The entire time, my tourists were riding in the van looking out the windows as if everything was fine. However, things weren't fine. I didn't want to weaken their confidence in their guide by pulling over and consulting a map in the first few hours of the tour, so I pretended to need some gas and I pulled over to a gas station.

"Where is the Hollywood strip?" I asked the attendant.

It turned out that I overshot the boulevard by miles on a side street. When we finally made it to strip and I told them what I knew about the Walk of Fame and Grauman's Chinese Theatre. I gave them about an hour and a half to walk around on their own and get lunch. I had accidentally wasted so much of our time in Los Angeles that we had to skip a few things in order to stay on our itinerary.

I caught up with Mike and we headed to Joshua Tree National Park, first stopping at a supermarket in Palm Springs where we bought groceries to cook at the campground later that evening. This was my first time organizing a shopping trip for international people who have never seen an American supermarket Mike and his group left first and he told me to follow the highway east and then turn north at the sign for Joshua Tree. Eventually, my group and I arrived at the park although Mike's group was nowhere to be found, and there weren't any of the park's famous Joshua tree cacti. I found a place for us to camp and showed the tourists how to assemble their tents. The Korean couple cooked that evening and during dinner I had a talk with the group about what to expect from the tour.

At the meeting, I wanted to appear confident, informative, and fun but I was nervous. I was looking into the faces of all of these people and I was sure that they knew I had no idea of what I was doing. I spent the first night as a tour guide wondering if I had made a mistake by choosing this job.

When I arrived at the Grand Canyon the next day and again met up with Mike, I discovered that I took the wrong entrance into Joshua Tree. Those poor folks in my group never got to see an actual Joshua tree cactus because I took them into the wrong area. We made the best of it though, and in the following days I realized that they just wanted to have a good time and see a few things along the way. They just needed me to play the leadership role, even if I didn't know exactly what to do.

That poor group had to be the experimental group. Throughout the remainder of the seven days there were various other mishaps. The van sprung a gas leak from a puncture in the tank and leaked a trail of gas onto the street for several miles. The loud Austrian girl and the quiet Vietnamese girl didn't get along and wanted me to mediate their conflicts. We arrived late to several more locations and I had made poor arrangements for some of our activities. That tour finally ended in San Francisco that Saturday and another one began the following day. As disastrous as it was, I dealt with each of my mistakes and by the end of the tour I was beginning to recognize a growing leader inside of me.

I worked for Suntrek from that first summer after college until starting graduate school and loved every minute of it. I became a leader and facilitated the adventure and fun for all of my clients, except for an unfortunate few whom I just couldn't satisfy. As a tour guide, I lived in campgrounds and hotels for years. I had no fixed address or phone. I slept on top of the van after the luggage and camping equipment were cleared and fell asleep under a sky of stars almost every night. Due to that position, I saw some amazing things and met some really amazing people. I spent a solid year leading tours throughout Mexico, which I absolutely loved. Overall, that job was the most satisfying, dynamic position I have ever had and ever expect to have.

Of course, the unfortunate part was that I could only live on the low wages for so long. I also couldn't live on bad camp and restaurant food forever. However, more importantly, although I was constantly sharing incredible experiences with groups of other excited people, I often felt lonely. It felt strange to not have any consistent companions. I would meet a group of tourists and spend all of my time with them for a few weeks and then I would have to say goodbye. That was never-ending cycle of life as a tour guide. The only consistent people in my life were other guides that I would run into in popular places like Las Vegas and the Grand Canyon. I also made a few friends at some of the regular places I would visit for activities or lodging, but it for the most part it was a lonely existence.

I signed up for the job for some travel and adventure after college, but the position also helped me recognize that I loved playing the leader role. Unfortunately, with the way things were set up at Suntrek, there weren't any possibilities for upward advancement. A tour guide can only look forward to being a senior tour guide. The few management positions were all filled by folks that weren't going to be leaving them any time soon, and any other available office positions would be filled by international interns on work visas. If I wanted to continue working in that field and actually make substantial money; I would have to begin an operation as a competitor. The rub was that if I became an entrepreneur with my own adventure travel company, it was likely that I wouldn't be able to spend all my time toting Germans to the Grand Canyon; I would actually have to worry about behind the scene aspects.

THREE DAYS IN IXPUJIL

I once had an epiphany that changed the direction of my life.

After I had been working for Suntrek for several months, I built up a comfort and a skill with the job. I also built up a confidence and a trust with the management, so they decided it would be a good idea for me to lead tours in Mexico. The management must be able to put full trust in a guide before they decide to place him in Mexico, because there are major differences south of the border.

First, tour guides working in Mexico only returned to the office in northern California once every three months. That meant that the guides only have contact with management once every ninety days. Also, tour guides in Mexico must be fluent in Spanish. Furthermore, the guides must have exceptional decision making skills and must be prepared for anything and everything. In the states, tours are easy: the roads are good; drivers only get pulled over when they break the law; all campgrounds have water and tables; grocery stores are abundant; and all businesses have a phone to accept reservations and answer inquiries.

Mexico, on the other hand, is entirely different and more complex. A guide has to have a complete table and chair set so that they can pull up to a beach and set up camp. There must be lots of purified water, which is usually purchased separately from food. For lodgings, the guide usually has to show up to campgrounds and hotels, hoping that there is room available. If there is availability, then the guide must haggle a price that Suntrek was willing to pay. Also, the big ass fifteen passenger van would often get pulled over by an underpaid police officer because either the tinted windows were illegal, the stop at the stop light wasn't long enough, the van shouldn't be on the road on that day, or for some other excuse. The Mexican police would always say, "I can either write you a ticket that you would have to pay at the bank, or we can take care of it right here, in cash."

I actually had fun dealing with the Mexican police. When I would first get pulled over, I would discuss with them in Spanish about how I felt that they were overstepping the boundaries of the law. Sometimes, once they made their inevitable offer to accept cash, I'd tell them that I didn't have any money but I could spare a few new t-shirts with the company logo on them. Amazingly enough they all seemed to accept the t-shirts as payment. However, my most successful strategy for dealing with the Mexican police was to pretend to not understand a word of what they were saying. Because I had a van full of tourists anyway, part of this strategy was to have them snap photos while I was talking to the police. I would still give them a t-shirt or two but, by not communicating with them and having a bunch of European tourists take their picture, the process went much smoother and was more enjoyable.

One day while driving from Palenque to Tulum, a trip that would normally take about ten hours, the van broke down. I had a van full of tourists in the middle of nowhere along the Guatemalan border and the van simply stopped running. I pulled over and tried to crank the engine and got nothing. I couldn't see any obvious problems with the engine; whatever had gone wrong was beyond my ability to repair. I had to assess the situation. There we were, broken down alongside a single lane road with no shoulders in the middle of the southern Mexican jungle. There was no traffic on the road and no sign of civilization. I hadn't seen a town for miles.

Of course my tourists were concerned, so I had to react quickly and with confidence. I took whatever food and water we were carrying down from the roof in case we had to wait for an extended amount of time. I told them that everything was cool and that I was going to figure it out. After all, "it's an adventure tour."

About fifteen minutes later an El Camino came down the road heading in the same direction that we were traveling. I stood in the middle of the road and flagged them down. I asked them how far it was to the nearest town and what it had to offer. Ixpujil was the nearest town, they told me. It was a half hour away although it didn't have anything: no hotels, no gas station, and no traveler amenities at all. They told me that the nearest town past Ixpujil was Chetumal, about an additional three hours away on the Belizean border. Chetumal did have a gas station and a few hotels.

I caught a ride with them to Ixpujil. I told the tourists just to sit tight in the van and eat and drink and I would be back as soon as possible.

I hopped into the back of the El Camino and rode for thirty minutes until we arrived at Ixpujil. It was a tiny, dusty town and I was dropped off right in the center of it. Looking around, I guessed the town had less than five hundred inhabitants. There was a small restaurant, which also doubled as a grocery store. There was an open-faced concrete building with yellow paint spelling out the word *Taller* and across the street there was a similar open-faced building with the word *Autobus* written on it. In the median of the two sides of the roads were a few parked taxis.

Everybody in town stared at me as I went over to the mechanics and asked them to look at the van thirty minutes down the road. I hired a taxi for the mechanics and two minivan taxis to pick up my thirteen stranded tourists. When we returned to the van, the mechanics looked under the hood and then under the van and told

me, "*Esta chingada.*" The van was fucked and it would require attention in their shop for a couple of days.

Three days, Fuck! I asked why it would be so long. They told me
that it was probably the major disk that broke, and that they would
have to go to Chetumal and purchase the piece before they could
install it. The installation would take an afternoon.

I got all of the tourists' shit from the top of the van, loaded them
and myself into the minivan taxis, and headed back to Ixpujil. We
were dropped off at the restaurant and I told them to hang out
while I figured out what to do. "What do I do with thirteen tourists
that don't speak a lick of Spanish," I thought. The tour was to end
in a few days in Cancun, so I thought that would the best place for
them to wait for me. They could stay in a hotel and get by speaking
English, besides it is beautiful and there is a ton of shit to do. I
walked over to the *Autobus* building and asked when the next bus
for Cancun was due.

"Tomorrow," the young girl told me.

Fuck.

The people could not stay the night in this town. There weren't
even hotels and we would have to pitch tents on the side of a dirt
road. I went to the taxi stand and asked what they would charge for
a trip to Cancun. It would be a twelve-hour trip for the taxi drivers
and they would have to take three minivans. I tried to bargain with
them, but they knew I was fucked. The total came to four hundred
dollars and the nearest cash machine was in Chetumal, so I had to
borrow the money from the tourists. I gave all of them the name
and number of the hotel they were to go to and told them that I
would call to make sure they were all right. I wrote the same information down for the taxi drivers. With a borrowed four hundred
dollars, they were on their way to Cancun.

Next, the mechanics and I had to organize a way to transport the
broken down fifteen-passenger van to their shop. We took two min-

ivans back down the road and brought some short chains. We attached a chain from the front of my van to one of theirs. The return trip took an hour because of the weight dragging on the min-ivan. By the time we returned, it was dark out, but they understood my time pressure and began to take the Suntrek van apart. Because I had absolutely nothing else to do, I watched them as they worked. I had dinner at the local restaurant and grocery store; in fact I had every single meal for the next three days at that place. Luckily the restaurant had a television so I was able to pass a good amount of the time watching horrible Mexican programming. As there was no hotel, when the mechanics finished I grabbed a blanket and spread out on a bench seat inside my van and prepared for bed. I asked them about the next steps and they said that we would definitely have to go to Chetumal for the part.

I awoke the next day to the sound of the mechanics working on my van. They had disassembled the entire thing. They jacked it up on a couple of cinder blocks on the dirt road in front of the shop. From the looks of the operation it seemed a bit ad-hoc, but from some of my other experiences in Mexico, and from what these guys were explaining to me they knew their shit. When the van was opened it seemed like a human body having heart surgery. They were right about the problem and showed me the broken disk. The disk was supposed to be connected to the bar that spun the back tires and propelled the vehicle. This disk was broke as a joke, defi-nitely *chingada*. Fucked.

There were two mechanics: the owner of the shop who was an older man with a great sense of humor and a hard working ethic and a younger man that had moved there only a couple of years prior after completing his mechanic training in the large, northern city of Monterrey. He was exceptionally bright and knew a shit load about auto mechanics and was an equally hard worker. These two guys worked well into the first evening and began again very early the next morning.

The second day was Sunday, and in Mexico nothing is open on Sunday. Rigid Catholicism coupled with low-paying jobs has created a culture rooted in weekday *siestas* and chilling on Sundays. The young mechanic, who was even younger than I was, spent a good portion of the day going to junkyards in the town to see if there was an extra part that would fit the bill. There was nothing. With nothing to do, I spent that entire day at the restaurant store watching television and drinking Nescafe.

By the way, why does Mexico produce some of the finest coffee in the world, but all you can get anywhere in the country is instant Nescafe? I asked myself that as I sat in the restaurant and thought about international trade.

Latin America, including Mexico, produces some of the finest gourmet coffee in the world, but rather than enjoy it themselves, they export it. Third World economies are usually very rich in resources, whether it's human labor, agriculture, or natural resources. However, the products they produce aren't necessarily enjoyed in those countries. China makes a ton of products that are shipped to the United States and then sold at Wal-Mart. It only seems fair that China should have a Wal-Mart too and that the Chinese should be able to purchase their own products. Similarly, Mexicans should be able to enjoy their delicious coffee, instead of just producing it and shipping it to the states. Economic disparity is a powerful force.

While I continued my thoughts about international trade, I began to drift off in the world soft drinks. There are certain products that make their way to consumers in the far stretches of the world. Coca-Cola is a great example of a global product. Who doesn't know about Coke? If you are alive somewhere in the world, the odds are that you have slurped down the tasty beverage. The logo is ubiquitous. I have been in the middle of the Darien gap, the jungle between Panama and Colombia, where indigenous groups with a total population of one hundred make their own clothes and live in makeshift structures. They know about Coke. I have been to the highland villages of Mexico, in the middle of nowhere where folks practice shamanism and get drunk and pass out in the town center for religious purposes, and they drink Coke.

In the tiny mountain town of San Juan Chumula in the state of Chiapas there is a church. Inside there are no chairs, no lights and no recognizable imagery just people sitting on the straw-covered floor. People from the community go to the church to visit the Shaman. Inside that church everyone drinks Coke. The belief structure with the people of San Juan is that they must burp to release some bad stuff within them and Coke facilitates burping. Coca-Cola has positioned itself in this community as a religious tool. Coke takes on a whole new meaning there. Anywhere there is a person, there is the knowledge of Coke.

What struck me at that moment is that, while I sat at the grocery store and makeshift restaurant, I didn't have access to the very product that was produced in that country. I did however have access to Coca-Cola, an American product.

The monotony of my day was broken up by a parade of sorts that lasted for a couple of hours. I am not sure what the parade was for, but the young mechanic invited me to watch it with him. There were decorated cars and residents marching through the streets. Mexico has a very interesting religious culture. Prior to the colonial conquest of "New Spain" by Cortez, Mexicans practiced paganism. Aztecs, Mayans, and Olmecs, to name a few of the major groups of people indigenous to Mexico, practiced multi-deity religions. As history tells us, Cortez boated his Spanish ass over to Mexico, and forcefully imposed the Catholic religion. An interesting mix of paganism and Catholicism was then born where many catholic saints took on properties of indigenous deities. The saints are recognizing and celebrated on different days and because here are so many saints, religious celebrations are very common. Because Mexicans are broke, the celebrations are usually limited to decorating cars and parading down streets. I guessed that this parade had something to do with some saint or another. I love Mexico. Although the parade was a nice diversion, the day concluded just as the previous one: asleep early on a bench of the van. All I could do was wait for Monday and hope that Chetumal had the part we needed.

On the third day, the young mechanic and I went together to Chetumal. It was early, and for some reason the taxi stand was empty so we hitchhiked for the three-hour trip, bringing the huge broken disk with us. The mechanic was used to going to Chetumal and knew his way around well. We were dropped off in the center of town at one of the major auto part shops. They didn't have what we needed. We proceeded to visit every auto parts store within walking distance, only to discover that none of them had the part. We then hailed a taxi and went to every auto parts store in town, again finding nothing. "Well, so much for getting a new one," the mechanic said as he directed the taxi driver to take us to a junkyard.

We went to every junkyard in Chetumal and again turned up nothing. I was getting very nervous because without this piece I could not operate the van and I really didn't want to have to think of alternatives. Meanwhile, I had a group of international that didn't speak Spanish tourists sitting in Cancun. If couldn't get the van repaired in Ixpujil, I'd have to have it towed to Cancun, which would involve getting a tow truck from Cancun to make the twelve-hour roundtrip journey. Then, I'd have to find a mechanic there and wait for them to install the new disk. The only other alternative was to call Suntrek management and have another van driven down all the way from Santa Rosa, California, a four to five day trip for them.

"*No te preocupes*," the mechanic told me not to worry. He had a plan C.

He told me that he was going to solder the broken disk together, so once again we returned to the town center to buy some solder sticks at the local market. I also went to a bank machine and withdrew as much money as I could, then we had the Chetumal taxi driver drive us back to Ixpujil. After passing through military checkpoints and a hundred bug ass speed bumps along the way, we returned after dark. He and the older mechanic began the soldering. The work had to be done precisely, and minor misplacements of the parts would result in the job not being able to be done. Therefore, soldering the disk would be a time consuming process. A couple of hours went by and it was very late. I invited the mechanics to the restaurant for some Nescafe and dinner. They took me up on a beer but had to go home to their wives and children. As it turned out, the young mechanic was a husband and father of two. He seemed more grown up and more responsible than I had ever been in my entire life.

As I again slept in the van that night, I really hoped it would be my final night of uncomfortable sleep. It had been three nights and I really wanted a bed and a shower and a decent meal. Also, I was really getting concerned about my tourists, and I had to worry about the new group of Europeans that were expecting me to begin their tour from Cancun to Mexico City in the next few days.

My fourth day in Ixpujil began early again. The mechanics continued soldering the disk at the crack of dawn. When I woke up, it seemed that they were about a quarter of the way finished and I thought it would be another long day. I spoke with the mechanics and although they assured me that it would work out and not to worry they seemed to be losing their assurance. I watched them for a while before going to the restaurant store for some Nescafe. I simply could not relax that day. I had been in the tiniest of towns sitting at a grocery store that nobody else except for me patronized as a restaurant for three days so far. For variation, I would walk around the town, which was nothing more than a couple of dirt roads. I walked back and forth from the mechanic shop to the restaurant every thirty minutes that morning to watch their progress. After a couple of hours, the hard working mechanics came to me and told me that they had good news.

Anticipating that they would tell me they were finished soldering, they instead told me that they found a used disk from one of their friends and that they were going to return to the original plan. I was the most relieved as I have ever been in my life, as they worked for the remainder of the afternoon replacing the part. By the late afternoon, they completed the work.

I thought about the work they had just done and the extent of my skills and knowledge, and it was this point that had a profound lasting effect on me. There I was, a college graduate, literally helpless in this situation. I felt so unskilled as I had to depend upon the mechanical expertise of these poor Mexican guys in this dusty town. I remembered some of the books that I had read and some of the discussions I had taken part in and some of the papers that I had written. I also thought about my skill base and my former jobs of cashiering and making pizzas. I looked at these two guys who had a mechanic shop constructed out of four concrete slabs and who lived in a town with dirt roads and no gas station and I became humbled.

Those guys worked their asses off and knew enough about automobiles to correctly identify the problem. They were incredibly resourceful and were going to get the job done at any expense. They worked long hours and dedicated themselves to fixing that van, just so I could drive some Germans to see pyramids. It was that point of my life when I became very appreciative and humble and realized that, although I had gone through a four-year college, I really didn't know shit. It was then that I knew I had to acquire some skills. It was then that I decided to further my education.

I thanked these two guys profusely and they asked for a fair price. I gave them double and I hopped back in the driver seat once again.

"BIG D"

As time passed the quality of the companies and the positions that I considered sharply deteriorated. I began my job search in areas that would be challenging and come with a nice paycheck. Rejection after rejection forced me to consider alternatives, until it seemed that there were no good alternatives. Every failed attempt at employment led to a lowered bar. I found myself considering selling ad space for a local newspaper and buying used cars for a living. I was applying to, and being rejected from, jobs that paid horribly and had zero opportunities for advancement. I had even been declined a server position at a restaurant in San Antonio, despite having a friend's referral.

When I attended the UT Austin job fair I talked to as many people as I could. I was determined to make some connections and was still walking around meeting representatives when everyone was packing up to leave. I quickly went over to one booth that was packing up and asked if they would still accept my résumé. They did. The representative, a young woman, asked when I was looking to begin a position.

"Immediately," I said.

She excitedly told me about a consulting position with a financial company in the Dallas area that may be a good match with my background as she asked me a few questions and wrote my responses on the back of my résumé.

"Tell me quickly how you solve a problem."

I explained that I would usually conduct research and, depending on what type of problem existed, certain analytical tools would be utilized to determine the severity of the problem and proper solutions. She wrote all of this down and asked me how I would analyze numerical data.

"SPSS and Excel are excellent programs for conducting statistical analysis, depending on what is needed," I answered.

She seemed excited to have met someone that would be able to begin right away, as most of the other job fair attendees were graduating seniors.

A week later, I received a call from a recruiter. She said that she had received my résumé and asked if I would be interested in business consulting. I responded immediately that business consulting would be my dream job and that I thrived in groups and loved testing the feasibility of ideas. For the very first time, the passion of my response was sincere. She asked a few more preliminary questions and then asked me to schedule another phone interview. "It will be intense," she said as I asked for recommendations on how to prepare. "You will go through a question and answer similar to most job interviews, but there will be a case analysis to assess your skills of logic. We are a results driven department and you will be presented a case, a problem, and you will have to respond with solutions and processes to implement the solutions on the spot. If you do well on the first phone interview we will invite you to the Dallas operations where you will undergo a four hour interview: two sets of interviews and two more cases to solve on the spot." We scheduled the phone interview for the next business day.

"I want this job," I sincerely told myself.

I loved statistics and making businesses more efficient. I spent that weekend looking over my research and statistics books to refresh my memory of various topics. I also informed myself about the company as much as I could.

The phone call came and I was nervous. I was confident that I knew my shit, but the pressure was intense. If I fucked up by forgetting some detail, or not mentioning a step or procedure, then I would lose my chance to proceed to phase two. On the phone, the interviewer was the same young woman I had met at job fair, which put me slightly at ease. She began with telling me more specifically of the position and then asked actual questions that were catered to the functions of the position in order to gauge my decision-making abilities. I shared my background and how I thought I was a perfect fit for the position. Finally, the last question was "tell me what you know about our company."

This was the first interview I had that asked me to share my knowledge of the company. Odd, because it always seemed fairly important to me that a candidate interested in employment be well informed about the potential employer.

Then came the hard part; the case. She read me the following case and asked me to respond immediately. There were two call centers, one in Los Angeles and one in Dallas. Customers contact them via email, fax, and phone calls. Recently, there had been a sharp increase in the amount of calls to sales representatives and twenty-five percent of them have been going unanswered. How would I solve that problem?

I knew that it was important for them to know that I knew methodology.

First, I would measure the amount of phone calls at each center and look for trends. It would be important to find out why calls were being placed, when they were coming in, and how long they were. To obtain this information, I would suggest monitoring the sales representatives. Each would be given a code sheet to indicate what the calls concern and categorize them. I'd then use this information to come up with a possible solution. For example, if all of the missed calls were within a predictable time window, then it may be necessary to make additional reps available during that time. Or, if many of the calls are concerning things that can be answered by the website than an automated customer service system may be the best solution. Any solution would also depend on the company's mission and goals too, I added.

As we concluded, she thanked me for my time and told me that they would get back by the end of the week. The wait is the worst part.

Friday afternoon came and, as always, the company underestimated the amount of time it would take to make the selection for the next phase. I called and spoke with the interviewer.

"We should have an answer for you on Monday."

I couldn't enjoy a weekend with this uncertainty looming over me.

Monday afternoon came and went. In my mind, I accepted the fact that once again I had not been accepted. I was not going on to the next round. I was beginning to get used to rejection.

That evening, I finally heard from the interviewer. I hoped for the best but prepared for the worst. The anticipation culminated to that point and my heart was pounding in my chest.

"I hope that you have some good news for me," I said after exchanging a bit of small talk.

"Jon, you have made it to phase two."

HOLY SHIT!

After seven long months of constant rejection, I had finally been advanced to round two! I was freaking out with excitement.

"How many other candidates made it?" I asked.

"Three, including you," she said and asked me to be at their office in Dallas at eight in the morning that Wednesday. They would reserve a hotel for me nearby.

"Of course," I said. Thank you for the call and the information, and I look forward to meeting with you and your colleagues."

I had a day. I used that time to prepare myself and know the company better than the chief executive. I spent the remainder of my free time refreshing myself on statistical analysis and research. I was going to be an expert on operational analysis.

It was a six-hour drive from San Antonio to the big D. I borrowed Breanna's car for the journey and brought my dark grey pressed suit, white and blue shirts, and a couple of ties. I had planned on wearing the white shirt, but accidentally bought one that required cuff links, which I didn't own. The ride north was nice. I passed the beautiful Dallas skyline, complete with modern skyscrapers and neon outlined buildings. A thriving, cosmopolitan center of commerce, Dallas is completely different from any other city in Texas.

I followed the directions to the hotel. I was expecting something cheap like a Motel 6 or Super 8, but the hotel turned out to be the finest hotel I have ever stayed at, The Westin. I rolled up wearing shorts and a t-shirt and immediately noticed that I was, by far, the sloppiest person in the vicinity. Everyone outside, in the lobby, and in the interior was well dressed in suits. The room was amazing. There were pillow top beds piled with a hundred soft pillows on a down comforter. I couldn't believe that the company had spent so much money putting up the candidates.

"Now, this is more like it," I thought as I realized that this was not only the first second phase interview I had been invited to, but this was the first time I felt that a company was going to spend any money to attract quality candidates. That night, I focused on preparation more than just chilling in the room. I prepared my portfolio, as I had done a dozen times prior, complete with my marketing and business plans, and statistical projects. I also went to half a dozen stores looking for cuff links but had no luck. The shirt decision was made; I was going to wear blue.

I couldn't sleep that night. I was excited and nervous. I wanted an offer so badly. I thought about all of the time I had spent preparing for the working world and had graduated at the worst possible time. I thought about how I would react if I didn't receive an offer. I was nervous about the performance that I was going to give the next morning. I had to outshine the other two people. I had to be confident, passionate, smart, and charismatic. That night, as the anticipation kept me from dozing off, I felt like a kid the night before Christmas anticipating presents in the morning. I finally fell asleep around three, awoke at six, and was tired as fuck. I was upset at myself for not being able to fall asleep and I was afraid that the sleep deprivation was going to negatively affect my performance.

I got dressed and arrived to the headquarters of the company, which was enormous. There were three buildings, several floors high that must have housed a few thousand workers, and a heavy stream of cars steadily pouring into the parking lot.

I made my way to the human resources department at seven thirty where I was given a lengthy application and told that all applicants needed to fill out the paperwork. They asked for the typical references, and signatures for the credit history and background checks. It took about half an hour to complete. There was one other applicant in the room: a young woman sat next to me busily scribbling into her packet.

At eight, the same woman that I had met at UT Austin and had interviewed me over the phone came into the room and greeted us. The other applicant and I were then introduced and I had met one half of my competition. Then, the interviewer left us for fifteen minutes to finish our applications. During this time, I had to learn as much as I could about my competitor to gauge my chances. With my skills at generating small talk and soliciting information, I discovered that she had finished an MBA in May, exactly as I had. I also discovered that her MBA was from the University of Texas at

Austin, a top tier university. The same university that requires entering MBA students to have two years of professional work experience, a 3.9 GPA with a business undergraduate degree, and a high GMAT score. Based purely on the differences in entrance requirements between our two schools, I felt defeated. She added that before going to graduate school she had actually worked as a business consultant; the very position that we were now interviewing for.

We were escorted to the third floor and were instructed to go into different rooms. I entered into a room with two young men. They introduce themselves and told me that there was also someone from the California office attending the interview via speakerphone. The two men were senior consultants and the woman on the phone would be the direct boss of whoever was selected. The interview began and mimicked the previous phone interview with the same style of questions, all designed by their group I learned later. "When was the last time that you had an epiphany," and "discuss a time where you displayed assertiveness on a team?"

The epiphany question caught me off guard and, instead of discussing my experience in Ixpujil, I ended up talking about the recent historical recall election in California where governor Gray Davis was voted out of office midterm. Not that it inspired much of an epiphany, but rather a realization that everything is malleable and dynamic. Even those that we elect through the democratic process can be recalled if the constituents deem them to be doing a haphazard job. I related the dynamics to and explained how I respected their business model because they also adapt and take a proactive role rather than a reactive role. I also went on to explain that, if hired, I would perform my functions with the knowledge that I could be replaced if there were a better performer in line or if I ever did a haphazard job. My responses were short narratives that illustrated me as both assertive and creative.

Then came the dreaded performance section. One of the two senior consultants laid a piece of paper in front of me. It was an integrated flow chart displaying decisions and who made them. They told me I had five minutes alone to study the chart and formulate a series of suggestions for them when they returned to the room. "I am sure that this will be similar to an operations class that you took in your MBA program," he said.

The pressure was intense. I had gotten all the way to phase two, had driven six hours, and had my suit pressed for this very moment. My heart began to beat fast and erratically. I was flustered and operating on three hours of sleep. I began scribbling all over the paper as to document my thought processes. I drew lines here, circles there, and question marks with phrases to remind me of what I was thinking. The great thing about pressure is that it has been proven to be an effective motivator. I finished, although I knew it wasn't my best work by a long shot. The two guys returned in the five minutes that they promised and I was still scribbling.

"Well, what do you have for us?" they immediately asked as they sat in front of me on the other side of the desk. "There are redundancies here and here," I pointed out, "which consumes time. This worker has a role where he can perform multiple functions in place of the one that he or she performs. The cycle here doesn't make too much sense to me and it seems that the process can be done in a timelier manner," I spit off as I walked them through my scribbles. The two guys shook their heads and jotted down everything on their papers. When that ended, they asked me if I would like to share any information about myself that I thought that they should know. I added, in part from advice that I had picked up along the way that I was passionate about the opportunity and, if given the chance, I assured them that I would excel. After two hours the first of two sessions was over.

Fifteen minutes later I was directed to the boardroom. I sat at a table large enough to seat at least thirty people and waited anxiously for the next session as I went over my responses in my head. Two people entered the room: a vice president of operations and another senior consultant. The process then started all over again. I was given a similar question and answer session followed by a problem to solve. This time, the problem was a quantitative one, which filled me with a little relief as my strengths were with numbers. This time, when I had my five minutes to prepare, I felt better, more awake, sharper, and more confident. It paid off that I sacrificed the last couple of days preparing for the analysis. I scribbled down a ton of shit. I drew out correlations, questions, and process suggestions. I was ready to shine when the two interviewers reentered the room and I blew them away.

The interview concluded at noon. Just before then, the vice president asked me to describe a time when I had to react quickly and independently to make a decision and I told him of my experience in Ixpujil. I walked away from the interview thinking that I was glad to be finished. That was the first interview I had where I felt that the interviewers actually got a good amount of insight into my abilities and potential. "The résumé is secondary," they told me "it is more important that you are smart and can adapt and act as an entrepreneur."

"Thirty-three percent chance," I said to myself as I mentally prepared myself for another possible rejection.

That was a Wednesday and they were to arrive at a conclusion early into the next week. Another weekend of being unable to relax with that uncertainty shit looming over my head. Based on the interview process and the strategy of the company, I believed that the company was tight. Therefore, I spent some of my weekend online and submitted my résumé to a few other positions they had open.

Monday eventually rolled around. I performed my usual routine: I woke up around nine, brewed some strong coffee, sat at the computer applying for jobs on monster.com, hotjobs.com, the University of Texas alumni job site, Southwest Texas State University job site, the Austin American Statesman, the San Antonio Express, and Craig's List. By that time it had been almost two weeks since I had heard anything from the car dealership. I gave the head buyer a call and was transferred to his voicemail. "Hello, this is Jon King and I just wanted to know of any updates and if a decision has been made."

That afternoon I received three notifications from jobs. The first was a call from the dealership recruiter in Houston that refused to take a look at my website. He quickly told me that they were going to move forward with other candidates. The second notification was an email. It was a brief message sent by a guy I had interviewed with for the alternative publication, the San Antonio Current. "Sorry, but that position has been filled," it said.

The third was also an email. It was from the financial company in Dallas. I curiously and excitedly opened it and it went on to say that "although [I] was a strong candidate they were not going to move forward with me."

At that point everything collided, my world collapsed. I got depressed. The dark cloud that had been hovering over my head for the past seven months had now become black, all because I couldn't seem to find a job. Every potential position had rejected me simultaneously on the same day. I had nothing. No interviews on the horizon. No network in place. I had just spent the last seven months being continuously rejected. I realized that the economy was going through difficult times, but why was I the one being constantly rejected? Did I lack the skills, was I too much of a generalist? I spent the remainder of the day curled up in bed fully clothed feeling like shit asking myself a million "why" questions.

When Breanna returned home, I told her what happened and she felt horrible. For over seven months she had been an ideal girlfriend: loving and supportive. She had always tried her best to get me to look at the brighter things that were ahead and promoted development of my interests and hobbies. It's the economy. It's the low wage city that we were living in. She pressed me to find work in other avenues, like part-time, just to have some income. She suggested that I do more pharmaceutical studies. She suggested that I paint, read, take pictures, ride my bike, and write. I did all of those things, but again the messed up thing about my life was that none of those things had any value at the time. All I wanted to do was work. Once I had a job, then I would concentrate on painting and writing.

That evening she convinced me to go to a nearby park that we had never been to and take a walk. She held my hand as we walked along the trails into the evening. Although I had a loving girlfriend at my side, that cared and loved me and assured me that I was in store for greatness, I continued feeling shitty. I really had no idea of what to do and I couldn't even think clearly any longer. I was at the height of my confusion. From dream jobs to shit, I had been rejected from every single position that I had applied to.

"What do I do now?" I asked myself, begging an actual answer but full of the same empty rhetoric that I had asked myself a million times before. This time was different though, there really had to be a change.

Should I return to school, and if so, should I try to get into a more prestigious one? Should I go for another master's degree or a doctorate or just take a bunch of classes in a discipline so that I would be able to teach? Should I continue doing what I was and hope for the best? If I went to school, would it be wise to deepen my debt? Should I again volunteer as an intern for no pay just so my résumé looks a little better? Should I move away from San Antonio, as my brother had suggested and move to Pittsburgh with him? If I left, how would I pay for the move? Would I find the same problems there if I did move? Could I sacrifice living with my girlfriend in a great house, for sharing a one-bedroom apartment with my elder sibling? It was obvious that something had to be done because nothing was working. I just didn't know what.

Fortunately for me, I had areas of passion that I believe many, in fact the great majority of folk's, lack. I loved economics and I was smart. My love for economics had always been a product of my hate of the global wealth disparity. There are a few very, very, very rich folks controlling eighty percent of the world's resources while the rest live in dirt-poor conditions. I have always loved to travel, and I have seen and spoken with some incredibly poor, in terms of monetary wealth, people; people without insurance, who make their own houses, who make their own clothes, who suffer from incredibly high infant mortality rates, who while extremely young perform the toughest manual labor functions, who lack transportation, who lack running water, and who are undereducated. All of who will never have an opportunity to visit my country or city a single day in their lives. Yet I, poor by American standards, can easily play tourist in their countries and their homes and take pictures of them so that I can brag to my American counterparts about the places I've been and the people I have encountered.

I also realized that the poverty levels are a global concern and are in our global control. American companies seek the cheapest means of production for whatever they produce within the boundaries of the law. American law protects Americans to an extent, although part-time workers and minimum wage earners, as documented in the book *Nickel and Dimed* by Barbara Ehrenreich, realistically cannot afford to live. In the book the author, a journalist with a doctorate goes "undercover" and shows that it is impossible to support oneself, let alone a family, earning minimum wage. When American companies seek workers externally the situation gets even worse.

What happens is that Third World citizens, kids and young women mostly, work their asses off in some messed up conditions, for some crappy pay. Then they either ship products to be assembled or perform the assembly there for whatever manufactured goods we are talking about. Those products are then sold at an exponential price to provide capital in the form of profits to American businesses. We have heard the argument in the past of "well at least they are providing jobs," right? Fuck that argument. American businesses have the pockets and the means to raise the bar. Americans, by doing so however would have to sacrifice their pay packages.

The global situation is also a factor of money and loans and the ability to recognize assets and capital. The International Monetary Fund with the World Bank is in charge of providing loans for Third World economies. The obvious problems are that the loans are only given with certain compliance measures, which force the capital to be spent in certain ways. Additionally there is no global legal system in place.

Well, having gone into all that shit, it brings me back to the idea of passions. As Breanna and I walked, hand in hand, discussing my predicament, I decided in part to pursue economics and eventually be an advocate for fair global trade practices. During that walk I decided to do the research on how I can do what I thought that I would love to do.

Our walk concluded and we returned to the car. I had left my cell phone in the car to recharge and when we returned around nine I had a message waiting. I listened to my voicemail and the message was from the financial firm. They instructed me to call them back. When I called them back they wanted to know if I still interested. I offered a resounding "yes." They told me that they would be in contact in the next few days to inform me of the outcome.

What I realized at that instant was that the rejection email from the financial company was not for the position that I had interviewed for, rather a response from the positions I had applied to online. Just like that, I became once again full of hope.

The next morning I turned on my phone and had another message waiting. Again it was the Dallas financial company telling me that I should give them a call at my earliest convenience. I called them back and was connected right away.

"Jon, we usually don't call in these cases; we usually send letters, but you have been through a rigorous interview process."

My hope was demolished; I knew that by her saying this, that it was a polite rejection.

"Also, you had some strikes against you with your lack of experience and everything."

I was convinced that the job wasn't a possibility at that point.

"But we would like to extend an offer to you."

Oh my god!

I couldn't believe what she had just said. I got the offer! I became overwhelmed and we finished the conversation. My heart beat fast, my eyes filled with tears, and I went into the street and screamed, "Yes! Finally!" At that one moment I became ecstatic. I was filled with happiness and joy. Colors suddenly became brighter and more brilliant. I started to cry. The depression, discontentment, and questions about my future evaporated in a moment's time. It was the single best thing in recent history for me. I called my brother within minutes.

"I got it," I told him.

I called my parents and Breanna. For the first time since graduation I had felt valued, and fulfilled and excited. Someone recognized my talents and it was for a position that I was going to love and that would be a springboard for bigger and better things. For the first time in months, I turned off the computer and went for a bike ride; the most beautiful, peaceful, relaxing, and exciting bike ride of my life.

A RHYME BY J-CURV

I have always been a fan of rap music for its irreverence and innovative nature. When I was a kid I wanted to be a rapper. I never pursued it, however I still enjoy writing rhymes. I wrote these in the midst of the seven months.

Two hundred hungry folks and only one steak,
So how are we going to divvy up the plate,
Equal slices would be just great,
But that's not how humans operate,
If you ain't got the skrill, back to the line andwait,
We all human, we all equals,
But we stratify our peoples, tell them be sure to check the peepholes,
We've turned reality into an all nude peepshow,
Don't get me wrong I'm not entirely a leftist,
But I do got a problem with the flashy skrilla fetish,
The cheddar, the clams, the loot, and the lettuce,
Dick Grasso, you're kind of an asshole,
Criminally greedy perpetuating the whole fiasco,
Businesses breaking workers off as little as possible,
Working folks living in poverty now how's that possible,
Workers are no longer temps at their transient positions,
But they got the temp mindset that facilitates their decisions,
Not to unionize cuz that would mean that they DO make fries,
And serve lattes,
But Starbucks treats their employees well don't they?

They are part-time with stock options,
But that's obnoxious cuz nobody can afford them,
Lets break down all trade barriers and set up global factories,
Where everything is produced by really poor Chinese,
And then shipped to Mexico so they can assemble it,
And then it's the U.S.'s turn to market it and profit,
And brand it, so consumers demand it, its outlandish, that,
You ain't ever going to get laid unless you wear Levis and Nikes,
You can't fly like Jordan with Reeboks but with Nike you might,
Real dreams may never materialize,
When we see the world with material eyes,
Pure capitalism can have hurting effects,
Like when the kid from Da Band got his first paycheck just to put the bling on his neck,
Hey if you are listening, listen to this,
Cheap prices mean cheap wages,
Not to say we should all run around naked,
But lets face it, multinationals are becoming our favorites,
Their model is tainted, they have too much control,
And now ALL manufacturers need Wal-Mart's say so,
Soon they will be THE ONLY kid on the block,
Eliminating ALL competitors first with mom and pops,
That means the only place to work and the only place to shop.

P.S. I ALMOST FORGOT

Searching—for everything that is already there, every thought already known, everything that ever will be. Struggling—oh how we struggle, and the more we avoid it, the greater the struggle becomes, until we realize that the struggle is the blessing.

—From hip hop artist Blackalicious, in intro of the album *Nia*

There is something within us all, some more than others, that tells us our jobs are an extension of who we are. Without a job you are nobody. We value ourselves according to what is printed on our business cards. At work we can be important. We can make decisions. We can play dress up and go to meetings. We also can collect a paycheck and pay for the food and clothes and rent, as we are modern day hunter-gatherers. With a job and money, we can feel good about ourselves because we have a place to go during the day. We have a purpose. During the 1930s, the United States experienced first hand the devastating effects that job loss can have on the human psyche. During the greatest economic collapse in our history as a nation an unprecedented number of men pretended to work when they had nowhere to go, and committed suicide because the depression was too much.

As a result of constant rejection, I experienced a lot of negative shit. My self-esteem was at an all time low, as well as my self-confidence. I actually took it as a reflection of my worth when I was being constantly rejected. "What's wrong with me, why do employers not want me?" I would endlessly ask my girlfriend.

Having no job means having no income. I couldn't afford to go out at all. I spent no money; in fact Breanna was supporting me the entire time by paying all the bills and buying all the food. She would lend me her car because I couldn't afford to fill the gas tank of my truck when I had to drive to Austin for a job interview.

I was depressed and angry. The world lost meaning. I tried to do the activities that I had always enjoyed like reading, bike riding, exercising, painting, and writing, but those activities weren't the same at all. In my mind was a constant thought on work that I couldn't let go of.

My father was a career military man. In the early '90s, when the military was cutting back spending, he was forced to retire. He had no idea of what to do with his time. He had invested so much of his life into his work that he simply could not accept the fact that he was no longer working. Being the resourceful guy that he is, he created his own work by doing automotive maintenance on his and my mom's car, and maintaining the house and the yard like a pro.

My grandmother in New York was laid off at the age of eighty. She lived to work. Having a routine and enjoying it can be essential. She worked because she loved it, not because she needed the money. There is something programmed in us that makes us uncomfortable with uncertainty; we want to have a routine. We need to produce and always set the bar higher each time. We have to push the envelope as far as we can. It's embedded in our genetics, and we are all living evidence that work and production pay off. All of our ancestors strove to produce and reproduce.

When I was unemployed, I never called anyone because I never liked talking about my predicament. Conversations would inevitably lead to a discussion about not having a job. I stopped calling the people in my life that mean the most to me: my brother, my mother, and my father. I could barely bring myself to call my father on his birthday and was relieved when I got his voicemail. I knew that I was drifting away from my family, but I really couldn't control it. I would tell them that I was sorry that I didn't call and I would explain that I was depressed. They all understood. In fact they all understood a little too well. They supported me the entire time by being understanding, lending me money when I needed it, and by offering their optimism on the future. Although I was more passive with them during this time, I needed them to be where they were.

I became a stress on my girlfriend. She would never know exactly who she was going to come home to. Would it be the happy, optimistic Jon who surfaced when companies would call him, or would it be the pissed off, depressed Jon who would come out after being rejected? Unfortunately she had to experience all of my moods. Throughout this ordeal, she proved to be the greatest woman ever. She held my hand when I needed it and gave me space when I needed it, but she was always there to try and help. I would have been lost without her.

For all of your support and appreciation, I love you all.

My advice to you all is not to evaluate yourself in terms of what you do on the job or whether you work, rather judge yourself using the important criteria: integrity, honesty, friendships, love, etc. Everything will eventually fall into place. Be proactive: spend some time looking and discovering where your passions are, spend some time appreciating the world around you, appreciate the friends and family that support you, and develop a hobby or a skill. But fuck it, the entire time I spent job hunting I was never hungry, I always had a bed to sleep in next to a beautiful girl, and I didn't have bombs blowing up outside of my window. What I am trying to say that even though it was bad, it really wasn't that bad. We spend the bulk of our lives on the job; enjoy the precious time that you are not at work.

And by the way, in case you were wondering, after I got my van fixed in Ixpujil, I drove straight to Cancun and reunited with my tourists at the hotel. It was great to see them again and finish the rest of the tour. They had a hell of a time.

0-595-32829-6